Simply Delicious!

COOKIES
brownies desserts cakes pies

CREATIVE PUBLISHING international

MINNETONKA, MINNESOTA

Copyright © 1999
Land O'Lakes, Inc. and Creative Publishing international, Inc.

Publisher: Pete Theisen
Editor: Mary Sue Peterson
Assistant Editor: Cindy Manwarren

For questions regarding recipes in this cookbook or Land O'Lakes products, call 1-800-328-4155 or visit us at our Web site at: http://www.landolakes.com

Chairman: Iain Macfarlane
President / CEO: David D. Murphy
Vice President / Retail Sales & Marketing: James Knapp
Creative Director: Lisa Rosenthal

Project Manager: Amy Friebe
Senior Art Director: Stephanie Michaud
Executive Food Editor: Carol Frieberg
Desktop Publishing Specialist: Laurie Kristensen
Publishing Production Manager: Kim Gerber

Pictured on front cover: Jumbo Candy & Nut Cookies (page 20).

Recipes developed and tested by the Land O'Lakes Test Kitchens.

Printed on American paper by:
 R. R. Donnelley & Sons Co.
10 9 8 7 6 5 4 3 2 1

Creative Publishing international, Inc.
5900 Green Oak Drive
Minnetonka, Minnesota 55343
1-800-328-3895
Printed in U.S.A.

Library of Congress Cataloging-in-Publication Data

Simply delicious : cookies, bars, desserts.
      p.   cm.
    At head of title: Land O Lakes.
    ISBN 0-86573-897-1 (hard cover)
    1. Desserts. 2. Cookies. I. Land O' Lakes, Inc.
  TX773.S525 1999   99-27799
  641.8'6--dc21

introduction

If you love baked goods as much as we do, you'll love the recipes included in this book. Inside you'll find indulgent sweets for special occasions and simple treats to brighten an ordinary day. Few things match the simple pleasure of freshly baked homemade cookies or a slice of just-picked fruit pie to celebrate the season. At Land O'Lakes we are committed to offering you the best of the best—we specialize in homemade goodness!

Inside, you'll find a fun variety of cookie jar favorites, brownies, bars and cakes which are a pleasure to bake and serve throughout the year. From cobblers and puddings to tarts and cheesecakes, you'll find delicious desserts to please everyone.

Just as important, these are recipes you can depend on. Each recipe has been tested by the professional home economists in our test kitchens. We've put them in easy-to-read, easy-to-follow format to help you produce perfect desserts with minimal stress and maximum satisfaction!

We believe that Land O'Lakes is a name people have learned to trust for quality. We are proud to offer you this collection of some of our favorite recipes and invite you to share them with your loved ones. May each recipe you try be "simply delicious!"

Strawberries 'N Cream Tart, see page 160

Table of Contents

Cinnamon Coffee Cookies & Macadamia Nut White Chocolate Chunk Cookies

Our Favorite Cookies

Rich & Chewy Bars

Cherry Almond Chocolate Bars & Chocolate Caramel Oatmeal Bars

Luscious Tortes & Cakes

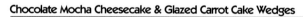

Chocolate Mocha Cheesecake & Glazed Carrot Cake Wedges

Favorite Pies & Tarts

Black Forest Pie

Irresistible Desserts

Individual Fruit-Filled Meringues & Salted Peanut Ice Cream Squares

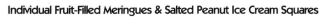

Baking Tips

Baking Your Best: Choosing the Right Spread Product for Recipes

Less than a generation ago, consumers had four choices to use in baking—butter, oil, shortening and lard. Today there is a bewildering display of over 60 types of dairy case spread products available at the grocery store. In addition to the several varieties of butter, there are margarines and spreads, plus diet and light variations. It is often difficult to distinguish any visible difference between these products, and choosing the right product may be critical to the success of a recipe.

The percentage of fat is the key point to check when selecting a product. Products with 80% fat are the only products, by law, to carry the name butter or margarine. Butter is made from milk fat while margarine is made from vegetable oil or a combination of vegetable oil and milk fat or animal fat. Products containing less than 80% fat are usually labeled spread.

Our recipes were developed using butter, an 80% fat product. If a lower fat product is used when preparing these recipes, you will not get the same results. Part of the reason or the failure is due to the higher water content of the lower fat products. As the fat content gets lower in a product, the greater the chance for a recipe failure. In general, spreads with less than 60% fat should not be used for baking or frying. They are intended to be used as table spreads. Spreads with a fat content between 60% and 75% will perform all right but may produce baked goods different from those made with 80% fat products.

Whipped butter and margarine, and soft tub margarines, are NOT to be used for baking, but are intended as table spreads only, due to their soft textures.

Unsalted butter and lightly salted butter can be used interchangeably in recipes. It is not necessary to change the amount of salt in recipes when interchanging unsalted and lightly salted butter.

For the very best results and flavor, use butter in your recipes.

(continued)

Baking Tips (continued)

Cookie-Making Questions & Answers . . .

Where should I place cookie sheets in the oven during baking?
For evenly browned cookies, place 1 cookie sheet at a time on the center rack.

What can I do if my cookies stick to the cookie sheet?
Warm the cookies in the oven for 30 to 60 seconds; remove immediately. Use no-stick cooking spray or shortening (not butter or margarine) to grease cookie sheets.

Why are my cookies spreading too much?
Cookies may be spreading too much for a variety of reasons. A test cookie will give a good indication of dough condition. Bake one cookie. If it spreads more than desired, the dough may be too soft. Try refrigerating the dough until well chilled (1 to 2 hours). If the dough is still too soft, stir in 1 to 2 tablespoons flour. Do not oversoften the butter before making the dough. Also, do not use low-fat spreads (less than 70% fat) in place of butter. Low-fat spreads have a higher moisture content and cause cookie dough to be too soft. If you have used a low-fat spread, go ahead and bake the cookies rather than trying to "fix" the dough. Another way to prevent cookies from spreading too much is to be sure to cool cookie sheets completely before placing more cookie dough on them.

What is the best way to cool cookies if I do not have a wire cooling rack?
If you do not use a wire cooling rack to cool your cookies, they can become soft or soggy. To prevent this from happening, place a sheet of waxed paper on the counter and sprinkle it with granulated sugar. Place the cooling cookies on the sugared waxed paper.

How can I make soft cookies? Mine are always too crisp.
- Do not overbeat the dough once the dry ingredients have been mixed in. Over-working the dough will toughen the cookies.
- Do not overbake the cookies. They continue to set as they cool.
- Soft cookie doughs usually have more moisture than doughs for crisp cookies. If your dough looks dry, add 1 to 2 tablespoons of milk, cream, buttermilk or sour cream.
- Cake flour will give a more tender crumb to your baked cookies.
- Excess sugar often results in crisp, not soft, cookies.

Dessert Garnishes . . .

To make desserts dazzle, your recipe needs to do more than just taste great—it must look special, too. Here are a few garnishing suggestions that will dress up your desserts for any occasion.

• Flavor 1 cup whipped cream with 1/2 teaspoon extract or 1 tablespoon liqueur, and dollop or pipe with a pastry bag onto pies, cakes, tortes, cheesecakes, etc.

• Chocolate shavings, curls or leaves make attractive garnishes for many desserts.
   • Curls—Warm a bar or block of chocolate in microwave on high until slightly warm (10 to 30 seconds). Using even pressure, pull vegetable peeler across chocolate. (Pressure will determine thickness.) Refrigerate until firm.

   • Leaves—Choose heavy, veined leaves such as lemon or rose leaves. Brush melted chocolate onto undersides of leaves. Refrigerate until firm. Carefully peel leaf away.

• Use holiday cookie cutters as stencils and fill designs with jelly or candy sprinkles to decorate frosted cakes.

• Place paper doily over unfrosted spice, gingerbread or chocolate cake. Sift powdered sugar over doily, then carefully lift off. Cocoa powder can be substituted for powdered sugar on white or yellow cakes.

• Pipe whipped cream or frosting, using a pastry bag or resealable plastic food bag. After filling plastic food bag, take care to snip off only one small corner for piping.

• Dip dried or fresh fruit or nuts into melted white or dark chocolate. Leave green leaves of fruit intact whenever possible.

• Crush candies or use small individual candies or cookies to decorate top or sides of cakes.

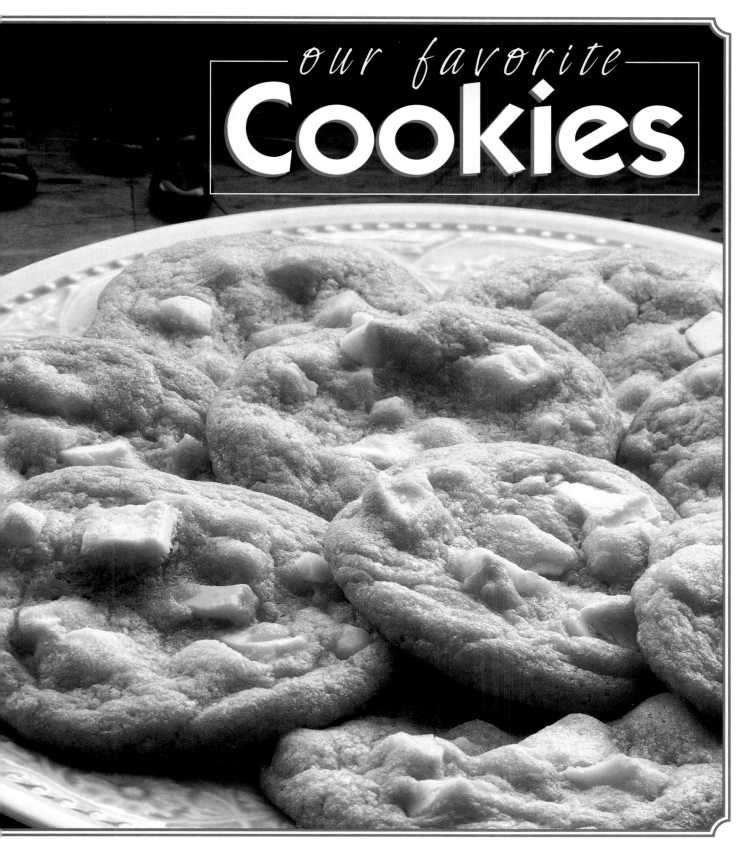

our favorite
Cookies

Cinnamon Coffee Cookies and Macadamia Nut White Chocolate Chunk Cookies

Cinnamon Coffee Cookies

*Coffee powder, pecans and cinnamon flavor these
easy slice-and-bake cookies.*

Preparation time: 30 minutes • Chilling time: 1 hour • Baking time: 6 minutes

Cookies

1	cup firmly packed brown sugar
3/4	cup LAND O LAKES® Butter, softened
1/4	cup orange juice
1	tablespoon grated orange peel
2 3/4	cups all-purpose flour
1	tablespoon instant espresso coffee powder
1 3/4	teaspoons baking powder
1	teaspoon cinnamon
1/2	teaspoon salt
1/2	cup finely chopped pecans

Glaze

1 1/2	cups powdered sugar
3/4	teaspoon instant espresso coffee powder
3 to 4	tablespoons orange juice
96	chocolate covered coffee beans or chocolate dipped pecans, if desired

In large mixer bowl combine brown sugar and butter. Beat at medium speed, scraping bowl often, until creamy (1 to 2 minutes). Add 1/4 cup orange juice and orange peel. Beat at medium speed, scraping bowl often, until well mixed (1 to 2 minutes). Reduce speed to low; add all remaining cookie ingredients. Continue beating, scraping bowl often, until well mixed (1 to 2 minutes). Divide dough in half; shape each half into 15-inch roll (about 1 1/4-inch diameter). Wrap in plastic food wrap; refrigerate until firm (at least 1 hour).

Heat oven to 375°. Cut rolls into 1/4-inch slices. Place 1 inch apart on lightly greased cookie sheets. Flatten slightly with bottom of glass. Bake for 6 to 8 minutes or until edges are lightly browned.

Meanwhile, in small bowl combine powdered sugar and 3/4 teaspoon espresso powder. Gradually stir in enough orange juice for desired glazing consistency. Spoon about 1/4 teaspoon glaze over each warm cookie; lightly press chocolate coated coffee bean on top of each cookie. **YIELD:** 8 dozen cookies.

Nutrition Information (1 cookie): Calories 45; Protein 1g; Carbohydrate 7g; Fat 2g; Cholesterol 5mg; Sodium 30mg

Macadamia Nut
White Chocolate Chunk Cookies

These crisp and chewy cookies are filled with
white chocolate and macadamia nuts.

Preparation time: 45 minutes • Baking time: 9 minutes

3/4 cup firmly packed brown
    sugar

1/2 cup LAND O LAKES®
    Butter, softened

1 egg

1 1/2 teaspoons vanilla

1 1/3 cups all-purpose flour

1/2 teaspoon baking powder

1/2 teaspoon baking soda

1/2 teaspoon salt

2 (3-ounce) bars white
    chocolate, cut into 1/2-inch
    pieces

1 (3 1/2-ounce) jar (3/4 cup)
    salted macadamia nuts,
    coarsely chopped

Heat oven to 350°. In large mixer bowl combine brown sugar, butter, egg and vanilla. Beat at medium speed, scraping bowl often, until well mixed (1 to 2 minutes). Reduce speed to low; add flour, baking powder, baking soda and salt. Continue beating, scraping bowl often, until well mixed (1 to 2 minutes). By hand, stir in white chocolate and macadamia nuts. Drop by rounded tablespoonfuls 2 inches apart onto greased cookie sheets. Bake for 9 to 12 minutes or until light golden brown. Cool 1 minute; remove from cookie sheets.

YIELD: 2 dozen cookies.

Nutrition Information (1 cookie): Calories 150; Protein 2g; Carbohydrate 17g; Fat 9g; Cholesterol 20mg; Sodium 120mg

Cherry Date Skillet Cookies

Snowy coconut coats these made-in-the-skillet, buttery date cookies.

Preparation time: 40 minutes • Cooking time: 5 minutes

1 cup LAND O LAKES® Butter

1 cup firmly packed brown
   sugar

1 (8-ounce) package chopped
   dates

1 egg

3 cups crisp rice cereal

1 cup flaked coconut

½ cup chopped maraschino
   cherries, drained

1 tablespoon vanilla

2½ cups flaked coconut

In 10-inch skillet melt butter over medium heat. Stir in sugar and dates; remove from heat. Stir in egg; return to heat. Cook over medium heat, stirring constantly, until mixture comes to a full boil (4 to 6 minutes). Boil, stirring constantly, 1 minute. Remove from heat; stir in all remaining ingredients <u>except</u> 2½ cups coconut until moistened. Let stand 10 minutes. Shape rounded teaspoonfuls into 1-inch balls; roll in coconut. **YIELD:** 5 dozen cookies.

Nutrition Information (1 cookie): Calories 80; Protein 1g; Carbohydrate 10g; Fat 5g; Cholesterol 10mg; Sodium 50mg

Buttery Pistachio Cookies

A delicious butter cookie filled with chopped pistachios.

Preparation time: 1 hour • Chilling time: 1 hour • Baking time: 10 minutes

1 cup sugar
1 cup LAND O LAKES® Butter, softened
2 eggs
2 teaspoons vanilla
2¾ cups all-purpose flour
1 cup (5 ounces) finely chopped salted pistachios, toasted
¼ teaspoon salt

1 egg white
1 tablespoon water
¼ cup (1½ ounces) finely chopped salted pistachios, toasted

In large mixer bowl combine sugar and butter. Beat at medium speed, scraping bowl often, until creamy (1 to 2 minutes). Add 2 eggs and vanilla. Continue beating, scraping bowl often, until well mixed (1 to 2 minutes). Reduce speed to low; add flour, 1 cup pistachios and salt. Continue beating, scraping bowl often, until well mixed (1 to 2 minutes). Divide dough in half; wrap in plastic food wrap. Refrigerate until firm (at least 1 hour).

Heat oven to 350°. On lightly floured surface roll out dough, half at a time (keeping remaining dough refrigerated), to ¼-inch thickness. Cut with 2½-inch round cookie cutter; cut each round in half. Place 1 inch apart on greased cookie sheets.

In small bowl beat together egg white and water. Brush tops of cookies lightly with egg mixture; sprinkle with ¼ cup chopped pistachios. Bake for 10 to 12 minutes or until edges are lightly browned. **YIELD:** 6 dozen cookies.

Nutrition Information (1 cookie): Calories 70; Protein 1g; Carbohydrate 7g; Fat 4g; Cholesterol 15mg; Sodium 35mg

Citrus Slice 'N Bake Cookies

*The flavors of orange and lemon shine in these
delicate butter cookies.*

Preparation time: 1 hour 15 minutes • Chilling time: 2 hours • Baking time: 7 minutes

Cookies

2	cups all-purpose flour
1¼	cups powdered sugar
¾	cup LAND O LAKES® Butter, softened
1	egg
1	teaspoon baking powder
½	teaspoon salt
¼	teaspoon baking soda
1	teaspoon grated orange peel
2	teaspoons lemon extract

Sugar

¼	cup sugar
4	drops yellow food coloring
2	drops red food coloring
2	tablespoons LAND O LAKES® Butter, melted

In large mixer bowl combine all cookie ingredients. Beat at low speed, scraping bowl often, until well mixed (2 to 3 minutes). Divide dough in half; shape each half into 6-inch roll (about 1½-inch diameter). Wrap in plastic food wrap; refrigerate at least 2 hours.

Meanwhile, in medium jar with lid combine sugar and yellow food coloring; cover. Shake until well blended (1 to 2 minutes). Remove 2 tablespoons colored sugar; add red food coloring to remaining sugar. Cover; shake until well blended (1 to 2 minutes).

<u>Heat oven to 375°</u>. Cut rolls in half lengthwise; brush with melted butter. Roll 2 halves in yellow sugar and 2 halves in orange sugar. Cut rolls into ¼-inch slices. Place 1 inch apart on cookie sheets. Bake for 7 to 10 minutes or until edges are lightly browned.
YIELD: 4 dozen cookies.

Nutrition Information (1 cookie): Calories 60; Protein 1g; Carbohydrate 8g; Fat 4g; Cholesterol 15mg; Sodium 70mg

Jumbo Candy & Nut Cookies

These oversized cookies are a family favorite.

Preparation time: 45 minutes • Baking time: 12 minutes
(pictured on cover)

1 cup sugar

1 cup firmly packed brown
   sugar

1 cup LAND O LAKES®
   Butter, softened

2 eggs

1 tablespoon vanilla

2 cups all-purpose flour

1½ cups quick-cooking oats

1 teaspoon baking soda

½ teaspoon salt

1 (16-ounce) bag (2 cups)
   candy coated milk
   chocolate pieces

1 cup coarsely chopped
   peanuts

Heat oven to 350°. In large mixer bowl combine sugar, brown sugar, butter, eggs and vanilla. Beat at medium speed, scraping bowl often, until creamy (2 to 3 minutes). Reduce speed to low. Add all remaining ingredients <u>except</u> candy and peanuts. Continue beating, scraping bowl often, until well mixed (2 to 3 minutes). By hand, stir in candy and peanuts. Drop dough by scant ¼ cupfuls 2 inches apart onto greased cookie sheets. Bake for 12 to 16 minutes or until light golden brown. **YIELD:** 2 dozen cookies.

Nutrition Information (1 cookie): Calories 330; Protein 5g; Carbohydrate 41g; Fat 18g; Cholesterol 40mg; Sodium 200mg

Chewy Jumbo Chocolate Chip Cookies

The addition of cake flour helps make these cookies soft and tender.

Preparation time: 45 minutes • Baking time: 10 minutes

3^1/$_4$ cups all-purpose flour

1 cup cake flour*

1 teaspoon baking powder

1 teaspoon baking soda

1^1/$_4$ cups sugar

1^1/$_4$ cups firmly packed brown sugar

1^1/$_2$ cups LAND O LAKES® Butter, softened

2 eggs

1 tablespoon vanilla

1 (12-ounce) package (2 cups) semi-sweet chocolate chips or chunks

Heat oven to 375°. In medium bowl combine flour, cake flour, baking powder and baking soda; set aside.

In large mixer bowl combine sugar, brown sugar and butter. Beat at medium speed, scraping bowl often, until creamy (2 to 3 minutes). Add eggs and vanilla. Continue beating, scraping bowl often, until well mixed (1 minute). Reduce speed to low. Continue beating, gradually adding flour mixture, until well mixed (2 to 3 minutes). By hand, stir in chocolate chips. Drop dough by ^{1}/$_4$ cupfuls 2 inches apart onto cookie sheets. Bake for 10 to 14 minutes or until light golden brown. DO NOT OVERBAKE. Let stand 1 to 2 minutes; remove from cookie sheets. **YIELD: 26 jumbo cookies.**

* 1 cup all-purpose flour minus 2 tablespoons can be substituted for 1 cup cake flour. (Cookies will be flat and less chewy.)

TIP: For 2^1/$_2$ -inch cookies, drop dough by rounded tablespoonfuls 2 inches apart onto cookie sheets. Bake for 10 to 12 minutes or until light golden brown. YIELD: 4 dozen cookies.

Nutrition Facts (1 cookie): Calories 310; Protein 3g; Carbohydrate 42g; Fat 16g; Cholesterol 45mg; Sodium 170mg

Chocolate Pixies

*Prepare the dough ahead and refrigerate; then bake
these chocolate cookies the next day.*

Preparation time: 45 minutes • Chilling time: 2 hours • Baking time: 12 minutes

1/4 cup LAND O LAKES®
    Butter

4 (1-ounce) squares
    unsweetened baking
    chocolate

2 cups all-purpose flour

2 cups sugar

4 eggs

2 teaspoons baking powder

1/2 teaspoon salt

1/2 cup chopped walnuts or
    pecans

Powdered sugar

In 1-quart saucepan melt butter and chocolate over low heat (8 to
10 minutes); cool. In large mixer bowl combine melted chocolate
mixture, 1 cup flour and all remaining ingredients except nuts and
powdered sugar. Beat at medium speed, scraping bowl often, until well
mixed (2 to 3 minutes). By hand, stir in remaining 1 cup flour and
nuts. Cover; refrigerate at least 2 hours.

Heat oven to 300°. Shape rounded teaspoonfuls of dough into 1-inch
balls; roll in powdered sugar. Place 2 inches apart on greased cookie
sheets. Bake for 12 to 15 minutes or until firm to the touch.
YIELD: 4 dozen cookies.

*Nutrition Facts (1 cookie): Calories 90; Protein 2g; Carbohydrate 13g; Fat 3g;
Cholesterol 20mg; Sodium 50mg*

Nutty Chocolate Chunk Cookies

Everyone loves these buttery cookies
chock full of chocolate and nuts.

Preparation time: 45 minutes • Baking time: 9 minutes

3/4 cup firmly packed brown
    sugar

1/2 cup sugar

1 cup LAND O LAKES®
    Butter, softened

1 egg

1 1/2 teaspoons vanilla

2 1/4 cups all-purpose flour

1 teaspoon baking soda

1/2 teaspoon salt

1 cup coarsely chopped
    walnuts

1 (8-ounce) bar milk
    chocolate, cut into 1/4-inch
    pieces

Heat oven to 375°. In large mixer bowl combine brown sugar, sugar, butter, egg and vanilla. Beat at medium speed, scraping bowl often, until well mixed (1 to 2 minutes). Reduce speed to low; add flour, baking soda and salt. Continue beating, scraping bowl often, until well mixed (1 to 2 minutes). By hand, stir in walnuts and chocolate. Drop by rounded tablespoonfuls 2 inches apart onto cookie sheets. Bake for 9 to 11 minutes or until lightly browned. Let stand 1 minute; remove from cookie sheets. **YIELD:** 3 dozen cookies.

Nutrition Information (1 cookie): Calories 160; Protein 2g; Carbohydrate 17g; Fat 9g; Cholesterol 20mg; Sodium 120mg

Nutty Chocolate Chunk Cookies; Cookie Jar Cookies, see page 28

Cookie Jar Cookies

Coconut, oats and rice cereal will make these crisp and tender cookies a cookie jar favorite!

Preparation time: 1 hour • Baking time: 13 minutes
(pictured on page 27)

3½ cups all-purpose flour
 1 cup sugar
 1 cup firmly packed brown sugar
 2 cups LAND O LAKES® Butter, softened
 1 egg
 1 teaspoon baking soda
 ½ teaspoon salt
 1 cup quick-cooking oats
 1 cup crisp rice cereal
 1 cup flaked coconut
 ½ cup chopped walnuts or pecans

Heat oven to 350°. In large mixer bowl combine all ingredients <u>except</u> oats, rice cereal, coconut and nuts. Beat at low speed, scraping bowl often, until well mixed (2 to 3 minutes). By hand, stir in all remaining ingredients. Drop by rounded tablespoonfuls 2 inches apart onto cookie sheets. Bake for 13 to 16 minutes or until lightly browned. **YIELD:** 4 dozen cookies.

Nutrition Information (1 cookie): Calories 160; Protein 2g; Carbohydrate 18g; Fat 9g; Cholesterol 25mg; Sodium 135mg

Cashew Butter Cookies

Salted cashew halves are an attractive topping
for these buttery cookies.

Preparation time: 1 hour • Baking time: 6 minutes
(pictured on page 31)

³/4 cup LAND O LAKES®
  Butter, softened

¹/2 cup firmly packed brown
  sugar

¹/2 cup honey

1 egg

2 cups all-purpose flour

³/4 teaspoon baking soda

¹/2 teaspoon baking powder

1 cup chopped salted cashews

Salted cashew halves

Heat oven to 375°. In large mixer bowl combine butter, sugar, honey and egg. Beat at medium speed, scraping bowl often, until well mixed (1 to 2 minutes). Reduce speed to low. Add all remaining ingredients <u>except</u> chopped cashews and cashew halves. Continue beating, scraping bowl often, until well mixed (1 to 2 minutes). By hand, stir in chopped cashews. Drop by rounded teaspoonfuls onto cookie sheets; top each cookie with cashew half. Bake for 6 to 9 minutes or until golden brown. **YIELD:** 4¹/2 dozen cookies.

Nutrition Information (1 cookie): Calories 80; Protein 1g; Carbohydrate 9g; Fat 4g;
Cholesterol 10mg; Sodium 70mg

Piña Colada Cookies

Pineapple and coconut combine with a hint
of rum for a delicious cookie.

Preparation time: 1 hour 30 minutes • Baking time: 8 minutes • Cooling time: 15 minutes
(pictured on page 35)

Cookies

1/2 cup sugar

1/3 cup
LAND O LAKES® Butter,
softened

1/3 cup pineapple preserves
or spreadable fruit

2 eggs

1/2 teaspoon baking powder

1/2 teaspoon salt

1/2 teaspoon rum extract

1 3/4 cups all-purpose flour

1/4 cup flaked coconut

Frosting

3/4 cup powdered sugar

1/4 cup
LAND O LAKES® Butter,
softened

1 teaspoon water

1/4 teaspoon rum extract

Toasted coconut, if desired

Heat oven to 350°. In large mixer bowl combine all cookie ingredients except flour and coconut. Beat at low speed, scraping bowl often, until well mixed (1 to 2 minutes). By hand, stir in flour and coconut until well mixed. Drop dough by rounded teaspoonfuls 2 inches apart onto greased cookie sheets. Bake for 8 to 12 minutes or until edges are lightly browned. Cool completely.

In small mixer bowl combine all frosting ingredients except toasted coconut. Beat at medium speed, scraping bowl often, until creamy (1 to 2 minutes). Frost cooled cookies; sprinkle with toasted coconut. **YIELD:** 3 dozen cookies.

Nutrition Information (1 cookie): Calories 90; Protein 1g; Carbohydrate 12g; Fat 4g;
Cholesterol 20mg; Sodium 70mg

Piña Colada Cookies; Cashew Butter Cookies, see page 29

Tart 'N Tangy Lemonade Frosties

*These cookies are reminiscent of a frosty
glass of lemonade.*

Preparation time: 1 hour 30 minutes • Baking time: 8 minutes • Cooling time: 15 minutes

Cookies

1¼ cups sugar

1¼ cups LAND O LAKES®
      Butter, softened

2 eggs

3 cups all-purpose flour

1 (6-ounce) can frozen
      lemonade <u>or</u> orange
      juice concentrate,
      thawed, <u>reserve 2
      tablespoons for frosting</u>

1 teaspoon baking soda

Frosting

3 cups powdered sugar

⅓ cup LAND O LAKES®
      Butter, softened

2 tablespoons reserved
      frozen lemonade
      concentrate

1 teaspoon vanilla

1 to 2 tablespoons milk

Yellow colored sugar,
   if desired

Heat oven to 400°. In large mixer bowl combine sugar, 1¼ cups butter and eggs. Beat at medium speed, scraping bowl often, until creamy (3 to 5 minutes). Reduce speed to low; continue beating, gradually adding flour, lemonade and baking soda and scraping bowl often, until well mixed (1 to 2 minutes). Drop by rounded teaspoonfuls onto cookie sheets. Bake for 8 to 14 minutes or until edges are lightly browned. Cool completely.

In small mixer bowl combine all frosting ingredients <u>except</u> milk and colored sugar. Beat at low speed, scraping bowl often and gradually adding enough milk for desired spreading consistency. Frost cooled cookies; sprinkle with colored sugar. **YIELD:** 4 dozen cookies.

*Nutrition Information (1 cookie): Calories 140; Protein 1g; Carbohydrate 20g; Fat 6g;
Cholesterol 25mg; Sodium 90mg*

Banana Cream Sandwich Cookies

These banana cookies are fun to make and are filled with a buttery
frosting for a delicious sandwich cookie.

Preparation time: 1 hour 15 minutes • Baking time: 12 minutes • Cooling time: 15 minutes

Cookies
2$\frac{1}{3}$ cups all-purpose flour
1 cup sugar
1 cup LAND O LAKES® Butter, softened
1 medium ($\frac{1}{2}$ cup) banana, sliced $\frac{1}{4}$-inch
$\frac{1}{4}$ teaspoon salt
1 teaspoon vanilla
$\frac{1}{2}$ cup chopped pecans

Frosting
3 cups powdered sugar
$\frac{1}{3}$ cup LAND O LAKES® Butter, softened
1 teaspoon vanilla
3 to 4 tablespoons milk

Food coloring

Heat oven to 350°. In large mixer bowl combine all cookie ingredients except pecans. Beat at low speed, scraping bowl often, until well mixed (2 to 3 minutes). By hand, stir in pecans. Shape rounded teaspoonfuls of dough into 1-inch balls. Place 2 inches apart on greased cookie sheets. Flatten balls to $\frac{1}{4}$-inch thickness with bottom of buttered glass dipped in flour. Bake for 12 to 15 minutes or until edges are lightly browned. Remove from cookie sheets immediately; cool completely.

In small mixer bowl combine all frosting ingredients except milk and food coloring. Beat at medium speed, scraping bowl often and gradually adding enough milk for desired spreading consistency. If desired, color frosting with food coloring. Put cookies together in pairs with 1 tablespoonful filling for each sandwich.
YIELD: 2 dozen cookies.

Nutrition Information (1 cookie): Calories 240; Protein 2g; Carbohydrate 31g; Fat 12g; Cholesterol 30mg; Sodium 130mg

Creamy Lemon Medallions

Tender lemon cookies are filled with a buttery lemon filling.

Preparation time: 1 hour • Chilling time: 1 hour • Baking time: 7 minutes • Cooling time: 15 minutes

Cookies

- 1 cup sugar
- 1 cup LAND O LAKES® Butter, softened
- 1 egg, separated, <u>reserve white</u>
- 2 teaspoons grated lemon peel
- 2 tablespoons lemon juice
- 1 teaspoon vanilla
- 2¼ cups all-purpose flour
- ¼ teaspoon salt

- 1 reserved egg white
- 1 tablespoon water
- Sugar

Filling

- 2¼ cups powdered sugar
- 3 tablespoons LAND O LAKES® Butter, softened
- 1 tablespoon grated lemon peel
- 1 tablespoon lemon juice
- 1 teaspoon vanilla
- 2 to 4 teaspoons milk

In large mixer bowl combine 1 cup sugar and 1 cup butter. Beat at medium speed, scraping bowl often, until creamy (1 to 2 minutes). Add egg yolk, lemon peel, lemon juice and vanilla. Beat at medium speed, scraping bowl often, 1 minute. Reduce speed to low; add flour and salt. Continue beating, scraping bowl often, until well mixed (1 to 2 minutes). Divide dough in half; wrap in plastic food wrap. Refrigerate until firm (at least 1 hour).

<u>Heat oven to 350°.</u> On lightly floured surface roll out dough, half at a time (keeping remaining dough refrigerated), to ⅛-inch thickness. Cut with 1½-inch cookie cutter. Place ½ inch apart on greased cookie sheets. With fork prick surface of each cookie several times. Meanwhile, in small bowl stir together egg white and water. Lightly brush surface of cookies with egg white mixture. Sprinkle lightly with sugar. Bake for 7 to 10 minutes or until lightly browned. Cool completely.

In small mixer bowl combine all filling ingredients <u>except</u> milk. Beat at low speed, gradually adding enough milk for desired spreading consistency. Put cookies together in pairs with about <u>1 teaspoonful</u> filling for each medallion. **YIELD:** 4 dozen cookies.

Nutrition Information (1 cookie): Calories 100; Protein 1g; Carbohydrate 14g; Fat 5g; Cholesterol 15mg; Sodium 60mg

Czechoslovakian Kolache Cookies

*A yeast-flavored dough is rolled, cut and filled with
fruit preserves for an attractive holiday cookie.*

Preparation time: 1 hour • Baking time: 10 minutes • Cooling time: 30 minutes

Cookies

¹/₂	cup milk
1	cup LAND O LAKES® Butter, cold
3	cups all-purpose flour
¹/₄	cup sugar
¹/₂	teaspoon salt
1	(¹/₄-ounce) package active dry yeast
1	egg
1	teaspoon vanilla
¹/₂	cup cherry preserves*
1	egg, well beaten

Glaze

²/₃	cup powdered sugar
1	teaspoon almond extract
2 to 3	teaspoons milk

Heat oven to 350°. In 1-quart saucepan heat milk until just comes to a boil; let cool to warm (105 to 115°F).

Meanwhile, in large mixer bowl cut butter into chunks; add flour, sugar and salt. Beat at low speed, scraping bowl often, until mixture resembles coarse crumbs (30 to 60 seconds). Dissolve yeast in warm milk. Stir in egg and vanilla. Add milk mixture to flour mixture. Beat at low speed, scraping bowl often, until well mixed (1 to 2 minutes). Divide dough in half.

On lightly floured surface roll out dough, half at a time, to 1/8- to 1/4-inch thickness. Cut dough into 3-inch squares. Place 1 teaspoon cherry preserves on each square. Bring up 2 opposite corners of each square to center; brush with beaten egg. Bake for 10 to 14 minutes or until golden brown. Remove to wire cooling rack; cool completely. In small bowl combine powdered sugar and almond extract. Gradually stir in enough milk for desired spreading consistency. Drizzle over cookies. **YIELD:** 2 dozen cookies.

* ¹/₂ cup of your favorite flavor preserves can be substituted for ¹/₂ cup cherry preserves.

Nutrition Information (1 cookie): Calories 170; Protein 3g; Carbohydrate 22g; Fat 8g; Cholesterol 40mg; Sodium 130mg

Snowball Cookies

*A favorite at Christmastime, pecan-filled Snowball Cookies
are scrumptious all year 'round.*

Preparation time: 1 hour • Baking time: 18 minutes

2 cups all-purpose flour
2 cups finely chopped pecans
¼ cup sugar
1 cup LAND O LAKES®
    Butter, softened
1 teaspoon vanilla

Powdered sugar

Heat oven to 325°. In large mixer bowl combine all ingredients <u>except</u> powdered sugar. Beat at low speed, scraping bowl often, until well mixed (3 to 4 minutes). Shape rounded teaspoonfuls of dough into 1-inch balls. Place 1 inch apart on cookie sheets. Bake for 18 to 25 minutes or until very lightly browned. Cool 5 minutes. Roll in or sprinkle with powdered sugar while still warm and again when cool. **YIELD:** 3 dozen cookies.

*Nutrition Information (1 cookie): Calories 130; Protein 1g; Carbohydrate 11g; Fat 9g;
Cholesterol 15mg; Sodium 50mg*

Chocolate Spritz Cookies

A buttery rich chocolate-flavored spritz with
a rich rum glaze for a creative flair.

Preparation time: 1 hour • Baking time: 9 minutes

Cookies
$1/2$ cup sugar
$3/4$ cup LAND O LAKES®
    Butter
1 egg yolk
3 tablespoons milk
1 tablespoon vanilla
2 (1-ounce) squares
    unsweetened baking
    chocolate, melted, cooled
2 cups all-purpose flour
$1/2$ teaspoon salt

Butter Rum Glaze
$1/4$ cup LAND O LAKES®
    Butter
1 cup powdered sugar
$3/4$ to 1 teaspoon rum extract
1 to 2 tablespoons hot water

Colored sugars

Heat oven to 375°. In large mixer bowl combine sugar, $3/4$ cup butter, egg yolk, milk and vanilla. Beat at medium speed, scraping bowl often, until creamy (1 to 2 minutes). Add chocolate; continue beating, scraping bowl often, until well mixed (1 to 2 minutes). Add flour and salt; continue beating, scraping bowl often, until well mixed (1 to 2 minutes). If dough is too soft, cover; refrigerate until firm enough to form cookies (30 to 45 minutes). Place dough in cookie press; form desired shapes 1 inch apart on cookie sheets. Bake for 9 to 12 minutes or until set.

In 1-quart saucepan melt $1/4$ cup butter. Stir in powdered sugar and rum extract until smooth. Gradually add enough water for desired consistency. Glaze cookies; sprinkle with colored sugars.

YIELD: 5 dozen cookies.

Nutrition Facts (1 cookie): Calories 60; Protein 1g; Carbohydrate 7g; Fat 4g;
Cholesterol 10mg; Sodium 50mg

Cranberry Hazelnut Biscotti

Toasted hazelnuts and dried cranberries combine to make delicious, crisp biscotti cookies.

Preparation time: 30 minutes • Baking time: 39 minutes • Cooling time: 15 minutes

2 cups all-purpose flour
$^1/2$ cup ($2^1/2$ ounces) hazelnuts <u>or</u> filberts, toasted, skins removed, finely chopped
$^1/2$ teaspoon baking powder
$^1/2$ teaspoon baking soda
$^1/4$ teaspoon salt
$^3/4$ cup sugar
2 eggs
$^1/4$ cup vegetable oil
2 teaspoons grated orange peel
1 tablespoon orange juice
$1^1/2$ teaspoons vanilla
$^2/3$ cup (3 ounces) finely chopped dried cranberries

1 to 2 teaspoons all-purpose flour

1 egg white
1 tablespoon water
Sugar

Heat oven to 350°. In medium bowl combine 2 cups flour, hazelnuts, baking powder, baking soda and salt; set aside. In large mixer bowl combine $^3/4$ cup sugar and eggs. Beat at medium speed, scraping bowl often, until thick and lemon colored (2 to 3 minutes). Add vegetable oil, orange peel, orange juice and vanilla. Continue beating until well mixed (1 to 2 minutes). Reduce speed to low. Continue beating, gradually adding flour mixture, until well mixed (1 to 2 minutes). By hand, stir in dried cranberries.

Turn dough onto lightly floured surface (dough will be soft and sticky). Sprinkle lightly with 1 to 2 teaspoons flour; knead flour into dough. With floured hands shape into 2 (8x2-inch) logs. Place 3 to 4 inches apart on greased cookie sheet; flatten tops slightly. Combine egg white and water; brush over top of biscotti. Sprinkle with sugar. Bake for 23 to 30 minutes or until lightly browned and firm to the touch. Let cool on cookie sheet 15 minutes.

<u>Reduce oven temperature to 300°.</u> With serrated knife, cut logs diagonally into $^1/2$-inch slices; arrange slices, cut-side down, on cookie sheets. Bake for 8 to 10 minutes; turn slices. Continue baking for 8 to 10 minutes or until golden brown. Remove to wire cooling rack; cool completely. **YIELD:** $2^1/2$ dozen cookies.

Nutrition Information (1 cookie): Calories 70; Protein 1g; Carbohydrate 10g; Fat 3g; Cholesterol 10mg; Sodium 40mg

Cinnamon 'N Sugar Shortbread

**This flaky shortbread is made extra special with
a sprinkling of cinnamon and sugar.**

Preparation time: 30 minutes • Baking time: 20 minutes

Shortbread
1¾ cups all-purpose flour
¾ cup powdered sugar
½ cup cake flour
1 cup LAND O LAKES® Butter, softened
½ teaspoon cinnamon

Topping
1 tablespoon sugar
⅛ teaspoon cinnamon

Heat oven to 350°. In large bowl combine all shortbread ingredients. With fork, stir together until soft dough forms. Press evenly on bottom of 2 (9-inch) pie pans.

In small bowl stir together topping ingredients; sprinkle over shortbread. Score each into 8 wedges; prick all over with fork. Bake for 20 to 30 minutes or until light golden brown. Cool on wire cooling rack; cut into wedges. **YIELD:** 16 cookies.

TIP: 2 (9-inch) shortbread molds can be used in place of 2 (9-inch) pie pans. Do not sprinkle with topping before baking. After removing from mold, sprinkle with topping.

Nutrition Information (1 cookie): Calories 190; Protein 2g; Carbohydrate 19g; Fat 12g; Cholesterol 30mg; Sodium 120mg

rich & chewy Bars

Cherry Almond Chocolate Bars and Chocolate Caramel Oatmeal Bars

Cherry Almond Chocolate Bars

A buttery pat-in-the-pan crust is topped with cherry preserves and almonds and then drizzled with a chocolate glaze for a very attractive and delicious bar cookie!

Preparation time: 30 minutes • Baking time: 20 minutes

Crumb Mixture
- 2 cups all-purpose flour
- 1/2 cup sugar
- 3/4 cup LAND O LAKES® Butter, softened

Filling
- 1 cup cherry preserves
- 1 (2 1/2-ounce) package (2/3 cup) sliced almonds
- 1/2 teaspoon almond extract

Glaze
- 1/3 cup milk <u>or</u> semi-sweet real chocolate chips
- 1 tablespoon LAND O LAKES® Butter
- 1/3 cup powdered sugar
- 1 tablespoon milk
- 1/2 teaspoon vanilla

Heat oven to 350°. In large mixer bowl combine all crumb mixture ingredients. Beat at low speed, scraping bowl often, until well mixed (2 to 3 minutes). Press crumb mixture on bottom of 13x9-inch baking pan. Bake for 20 to 25 minutes or until edges are lightly browned.

In same mixer bowl stir together all filling ingredients. Spread filling over hot crust.

In 1-quart saucepan melt chocolate chips and 1 tablespoon butter over low heat, stirring occasionally, until smooth (2 to 3 minutes). Stir in all remaining glaze ingredients. Drizzle warm glaze over bars. Cool completely; cut into bars. **YIELD:** 36 bars.

Nutrition Information (1 bar): Calories 120; Protein 1g; Carbohydrate 16g; Fat 6g; Cholesterol 10mg; Sodium 45mg

Chocolate Caramel Oatmeal Bars

These chewy caramel bars are utterly delicious.

Preparation time: 45 minutes • Baking time: 28 minutes • Cooling time: 1 hour

Crumb Mixture
1½ cups all-purpose flour
 1 cup quick-cooking oats
 1 cup firmly packed brown sugar
¾ cup LAND O LAKES® Butter, softened
¾ teaspoon baking soda
½ teaspoon salt

Caramel Mixture
½ cup milk
 1 (14-ounce) package (48) caramels, unwrapped

Filling
 1 cup semi-sweet real chocolate chips
½ cup chopped pecans

Topping
 1 cup semi-sweet real chocolate chips, melted
 60 (about 5 ounces) pecan halves

Heat oven to 350°. In large mixer bowl combine all crumb mixture ingredients. Beat at medium speed, scraping bowl often, until mixture is crumbly (2 to 3 minutes). Reserve 1 cup crumb mixture; set aside. Press remaining mixture on bottom of 13x9-inch baking pan. Bake for 10 minutes.

Meanwhile, in 2-quart saucepan combine milk and caramels. Cook over medium low heat, stirring occasionally, until caramels melt and mixture is creamy (15 to 20 minutes). Sprinkle hot partially baked crust with 1 cup chocolate chips and ½ cup chopped pecans. Pour caramel mixture evenly over chocolate chips and pecans. Sprinkle with reserved crumb mixture; pat lightly. Bake for 18 to 22 minutes or until caramel is bubbly around edges. Cool completely; cut into bars.

On each bar, place ½ teaspoon melted chocolate; top with pecan half. Store in tightly covered container. **YIELD:** 60 bars.

Nutrition Information (1 bar): Calories 130; Protein 1g; Carbohydrate 16g; Fat 7g; Cholesterol 5mg; Sodium 70mg

Chocolate Caramel & Nut Treats

*Popular caramel, chocolate and peanuts combine to make
a treat kids of all ages will enjoy.*

Preparation time: 15 minutes • Cooking time: 8 minutes

12   double (5x2½-inch) graham
crackers
¾   cup firmly packed brown
sugar
¾   cup LAND O LAKES® Butter
1   (6-ounce) package (1 cup)
semi-sweet real chocolate
chips
1   cup salted peanuts

Line 15x10x1-inch jelly roll pan with graham crackers. In 2-quart saucepan combine sugar and butter. Cook over medium heat, stirring occasionally, until mixture comes to a full boil (3 to 5 minutes). Boil, stirring constantly, 5 minutes. Immediately pour over graham crackers; spread to coat. Sprinkle with chocolate chips. Let stand 1 minute; spread chocolate chips. Sprinkle with peanuts; lightly press peanuts into chocolate. Cool completely; break into pieces. **YIELD:** 48 bars.

*Nutrition Information (1 bar): Calories 100; Protein 1g; Carbohydrate 11g; Fat 6g;
Cholesterol 10mg; Sodium 110mg*

Microwave Toffee Bars

*Chocolate and peanut butter team up in this
easy microwave recipe.*

Preparation time: 20 minutes • Microwave time: 8 minutes • Chilling time: 1 hour 30 minutes

5½ double (5x2½-inch)
    graham crackers

1 cup (6 double 5x2½-inch)
    crushed graham crackers

¾ cup sugar

½ cup firmly packed brown
    sugar

½ cup LAND O LAKES® Butter

⅓ cup milk

½ cup semi-sweet real
    chocolate chips

¼ cup chunky-style peanut
    butter

Line bottom of buttered 12x8-inch baking dish with graham crackers; set aside. In 2-quart casserole combine all remaining ingredients <u>except</u> chocolate chips and peanut butter. Microwave on HIGH, stirring after half the time, until mixture comes to a full boil (2 to 2½ minutes). Microwave on HIGH 5 minutes (mixture will be very hot). Immediately pour mixture evenly over crackers. In 2-cup glass measure combine chocolate chips and peanut butter. Microwave on HIGH until chocolate is softened (45 to 60 seconds). Stir until smooth and melted. Spread evenly over toffee mixture; refrigerate until chocolate is set (at least 1½ hours). Cut into bars; store at room temperature. **YIELD:** 32 bars.

*Nutrition Information (1 bar): Calories 100; Protein 1g; Carbohydrate 14g; Fat 5g;
Cholesterol 10mg; Sodium 75mg*

Orange Butter Cream Squares

This creamy bar cookie combines two favorite flavors - orange and chocolate.

Preparation time: 30 minutes • Chilling time: 2 hours

Crust
1¼ cups (about 25) finely crushed chocolate wafer cookies

⅓ cup LAND O LAKES® Butter, softened

Filling
1½ cups powdered sugar

⅓ cup LAND O LAKES® Butter, softened

2 teaspoons grated orange peel

1 tablespoon milk

½ teaspoon vanilla

Glaze
1 tablespoon LAND O LAKES® Butter, melted

1 tablespoon unsweetened cocoa

In medium bowl stir together all crust ingredients. Press on bottom of 8- or 9-inch square pan. Cover; refrigerate until firm (1 hour).

In small mixer bowl combine all filling ingredients. Beat at medium speed, scraping bowl often, until creamy (3 to 4 minutes). Spread over crust.

In small bowl combine all glaze ingredients; drizzle over filling. Refrigerate until firm (1 to 2 hours). Cut into bars; store refrigerated. **YIELD:** 25 bars.

Nutrition Information (1 bar): Calories 90; Protein 1g; Carbohydrate 10g; Fat 6g; Cholesterol 15mg; Sodium 85mg

Chewy Candy Crunch Bars

A chewy caramel coats crisp cereal in this sure-to-please bar.

Preparation time: 20 minutes • Cooking time: 5 minutes

4 cups bite-size crispy corn
   cereal squares
1 cup salted peanuts
1 (8-ounce) package (1 cup)
   candy coated milk
   chocolate pieces
$^1/_2$ cup LAND O LAKES® Butter
1 cup firmly packed brown
   sugar
$^1/_2$ cup light corn syrup
2 tablespoons all-purpose
   flour

In large bowl combine cereal, peanuts and candies; set aside. In 2-quart saucepan melt butter (2 to 4 minutes). Stir in all remaining ingredients. Cook over medium heat, stirring occasionally, until mixture comes to a full boil (2 to 4 minutes). Boil 1 minute. Pour over cereal mixture; toss to coat well. Press on bottom of buttered 13x9-inch pan. Cool completely; cut into bars. **YIELD:** 36 bars.

*Nutrition Information (1 bar): Calories 130; Protein 2g; Carbohydrate 18g; Fat 6g;
Cholesterol 8mg; Sodium 100mg*

Chewy Candy Crunch Bars; Chocolate-Topped Crunchy Cereal Bars, see page 60

Chocolate-Topped Crunchy Cereal Bars

Immediately sprinkle chocolate chips over the hot cereal mixture for an easy chocolate frosting.

Preparation time: 20 minutes • Cooking time: 10 minutes • Chilling time: 30 minutes
(pictured on page 59)

1 cup sugar
1/2 cup all-purpose flour
1/2 cup LAND O LAKES® Butter
2/3 cup light corn syrup
1/3 cup milk
4 cups toasted graham cereal squares
3 cups crisp rice cereal
1 cup salted peanuts
1 1/2 cups semi-sweet real chocolate chips

In 6-quart Dutch oven combine sugar, flour, butter, corn syrup and milk. Cook over medium heat, stirring occasionally, until mixture comes to a full boil (5 to 8 minutes). Boil, stirring constantly, 5 minutes. Remove from heat; stir in cereals and peanuts until well coated. Spread into 13x9-inch pan. Immediately sprinkle with chocolate chips. Let stand 4 minutes; spread chocolate chips. Cover; refrigerate until firm (at least 30 minutes). Cut into bars.
YIELD: 36 bars.

Nutrition Information (1 bar): Calories 150; Protein 2g; Carbohydrate 21g; Fat 7g; Cholesterol 7mg; Sodium 130mg

Chocolate Drizzled Cherry Bars

The favorite combination of chocolate and cherry
makes these bars delicious.

Preparation time: 30 minutes • Baking time: 42 minutes
(pictured on page 63)

Crumb Mixture
2 cups all-purpose flour
2 cups quick-cooking oats
1½ cups sugar
1¼ cups LAND O LAKES® Butter, softened

Filling
1 (21-ounce) can cherry fruit filling
1 teaspoon almond extract

Glaze
½ cup semi-sweet real chocolate chips
1 tablespoon shortening

Heat oven to 350°. In large mixer bowl combine all crumb mixture ingredients. Beat at low speed, scraping bowl often, until mixture is crumbly (1 to 2 minutes). Reserve 1½ cups crumb mixture; press remaining crumb mixture on bottom of 13x9-inch baking pan. Bake for 15 to 20 minutes or until edges are very lightly browned.

Meanwhile, in same bowl stir together fruit filling and almond extract. Spread filling over hot partially baked crust; sprinkle with reserved crumb mixture. Continue baking for 27 to 32 minutes or until lightly browned.

In 1-quart saucepan melt chocolate chips and shortening over low heat, stirring occasionally, until smooth (2 to 3 minutes). Drizzle glaze over bars. Cool completely; cut into bars.
YIELD: 36 bars.

TIP: Bars can be cut into shapes other than squares and rectangles. Try cutting into diamonds or triangles for gift giving.

Nutrition Information (1 bar): Calories 160; Protein 2g; Carbohydrate 22g; Fat 8g;
Cholesterol 15mg; Sodium 70mg

Applesauce Raisin Bars

This moist and buttery applesauce bar is topped with
a fluffy butter pecan frosting.

Preparation time: 30 minutes • Baking time: 25 minutes • Cooling time: 1 hour
(pictured on page 105)

Bars
1	cup sugar
1/3	cup LAND O LAKES® Butter, softened
1	egg
1½	cups all-purpose flour
1½	cups applesauce
1	teaspoon allspice
1	teaspoon cinnamon
¾	teaspoon baking soda
½	teaspoon salt
½	cup raisins

Frosting
¼	cup LAND O LAKES® Butter, softened
2	cups powdered sugar
⅛	teaspoon allspice
⅛	teaspoon cinnamon
2	tablespoons milk
2	teaspoons vanilla
½	cup chopped pecans

Heat oven to 350°. In large mixer bowl combine sugar, 1/3 cup butter and egg. Beat at medium speed, scraping bowl often, until creamy (1 to 2 minutes). Reduce speed to low; add flour, applesauce, allspice, cinnamon, baking soda and salt. Continue beating, scraping bowl often, until well mixed (2 to 3 minutes). By hand, stir in raisins. Spoon batter into greased 13x9-inch baking pan. Bake for 25 to 35 minutes or until toothpick inserted in center comes out clean. Cool completely.

In small mixer bowl combine all frosting ingredients <u>except</u> pecans. Beat at medium speed, scraping bowl often, until smooth (1 to 2 minutes). By hand, gently stir in pecans. Frost cooled bars; cut into bars. **YIELD:** 48 bars.

Nutrition Information (1 bar): Calories 80; Protein 1g; Carbohydrate 14g; Fat 3g; Cholesterol 10mg; Sodium 65mg

Applesauce Raisin Bars; Chocolate Drizzled Cherry Bars, see page 61

Peanut Butter Chocolate Bars

These bars are "heavenly" good.

Preparation time: 30 minutes • Baking time: 40 minutes

Crust

- 1 cup all-purpose flour
- 1/3 cup sugar
- 1/2 cup LAND O LAKES® Butter, softened

Filling

- 1/2 cup sugar
- 1/4 cup crunchy-style peanut butter
- 1/2 cup light corn syrup
- 2 eggs
- 1/4 teaspoon salt
- 1/2 teaspoon vanilla
- 1/2 cup semi-sweet chocolate chips
- 1/2 cup flaked coconut

Heat oven to 350°. In small mixer bowl combine all crust ingredients. Beat at low speed, scraping bowl often, until mixture is crumbly (1 to 2 minutes). Press on bottom of greased 8- or 9-inch square baking pan. Bake for 15 to 20 minutes or until edges are lightly browned.

Meanwhile, in same mixer bowl combine all filling ingredients except chocolate chips and coconut. Beat at low speed, scraping bowl often, until well mixed (1 to 2 minutes). By hand, stir in chocolate chips and coconut; pour over hot partially baked crust. Continue baking for 25 to 30 minutes or until filling is set and golden brown. Cool completely; cut into bars. **YIELD:** 25 bars.

Nutrition Information (1 bar): Calories 140; Protein 2g; Carbohydrate 19g; Fat 7g; Cholesterol 27mg; Sodium 82mg

Caramel 'N Chocolate Pecan Bars

Popular candy flavors combined in an easy bar.

Preparation time: 30 minutes • Baking time: 18 minutes

Crust

- 2 cups all-purpose flour
- 1 cup firmly packed brown sugar
- 1/2 cup LAND O LAKES® Butter, softened

- 1 cup pecan halves

Caramel Layer

- 2/3 cup LAND O LAKES® Butter
- 1/2 cup firmly packed brown sugar

- 1 (6-ounce) package (1 cup) semi-sweet real chocolate chips

Heat oven to 350°. In large mixer bowl combine all crust ingredients <u>except</u> pecans. Beat at medium speed, scraping bowl often, until well mixed and particles are fine (2 to 3 minutes). Press on bottom of 13x9-inch baking pan. Sprinkle pecans evenly over unbaked crust.

In 1-quart saucepan combine 2/3 cup butter and 1/2 cup brown sugar. Cook over medium heat, stirring constantly, until mixture comes to a full boil. Boil, stirring constantly, until candy thermometer reaches 242°F or small amount of mixture dropped into ice water forms a firm ball (about 1 minute). Pour evenly over pecans and crust. Bake for 18 to 22 minutes or until entire caramel layer is bubbly. Remove from oven. Sprinkle with chocolate chips; let stand 2 to 3 minutes. With knife, swirl chips leaving some whole for marbled effect. Cool completely; cut into bars. **YIELD:** 36 bars.

Nutrition Information (1 bar): Calories 160; Protein 1g; Carbohydrate 18g; Fat 10g; Cholesterol 15mg; Sodium 65mg

Peanut Chocolate Swirl Bars

These blonde brownies are swirled with chocolate chips and peanuts.

Preparation time: 25 minutes • Baking time: 18 minutes

1/2 cup LAND O LAKES® Butter
2 cups firmly packed brown sugar
2 teaspoons vanilla
2 eggs
1 1/2 cups all-purpose flour
2 teaspoons baking powder
1/2 teaspoon salt
1 cup chopped salted peanuts
1 cup semi-sweet chocolate chips

Heat oven to 350°. In 3-quart saucepan melt butter over medium heat (3 to 5 minutes). Remove from heat. Stir in brown sugar, vanilla and eggs. Stir in flour, baking powder and salt. Stir in peanuts and chocolate chips. Spread into greased 13x9-inch baking pan. (Chips will melt slightly and give a swirled effect.) Bake for 18 to 25 minutes or until firm to the touch. DO NOT OVERBAKE. Cool completely; cut into bars. **YIELD:** 36 bars.

Nutrition Facts (1 bar): Calories 140; Protein 2g; Carbohydrate 19g; Fat 7g; Cholesterol 20mg; Sodium 100mg

Caramel Rocky Road Bars

Caramel, peanut, marshmallow and chocolate lovers,
BEWARE—these bars may be deliciously habit-forming!

Preparation time: 30 minutes • Baking time: 32 minutes • Chilling time: 1 hour

Crumb Mixture
1 cup all-purpose flour
$3/4$ cup quick-cooking oats
$1/2$ cup sugar
$1/2$ cup LAND O LAKES®
    Butter, softened
$1/2$ teaspoon baking soda
$1/4$ teaspoon salt
$1/4$ cup chopped salted peanuts

Filling
$1/2$ cup caramel ice cream
    topping
$1/2$ cup salted peanuts
$1 1/2$ cups miniature
    marshmallows
$1/2$ cup milk chocolate chips

Heat oven to 350°. In small mixer bowl combine all crumb mixture ingredients <u>except</u> chopped peanuts. Beat at low speed, scraping bowl often, until mixture is crumbly (1 to 2 minutes). By hand, stir in $1/4$ cup peanuts. <u>Reserve $3/4$ cup crumb mixture</u>; set aside. Press remaining crumb mixture on bottom of greased and floured 8- or 9-inch square baking pan. Bake for 12 to 17 minutes or until lightly browned.

Spread caramel topping evenly over hot partially baked crust. Sprinkle with $1/2$ cup peanuts, marshmallows and chocolate chips. Crumble reserved crumb mixture over chocolate chips. Continue baking for 20 to 25 minutes or until crumb mixture is lightly browned. Refrigerate until firm (at least 1 hour). Cut into bars. **YIELD:** 25 bars.

Nutrition Information (1 bar): Calories 120; Protein 2g; Carbohydrate 16g; Fat 6g;
Cholesterol 10mg; Sodium 120mg

Peanut Brittle Bars

These bars are reminiscent of an old-fashioned candy.

Preparation time: 30 minutes • Baking time: 15 minutes • Cooling time: 30 minutes

Bars
- 1 cup sugar
- 1 cup LAND O LAKES® Butter, softened
- 1/2 teaspoon salt
- 1 teaspoon vanilla
- 2 cups all-purpose flour
- 1 cup salted peanuts <u>or</u> chopped salted cashews
- 1 (6-ounce) package (1 cup) semi-sweet real chocolate chips

Glaze
- 1 cup powdered sugar
- 2 tablespoons creamy peanut butter
- 2 to 3 tablespoons hot water

Heat oven to 375°. In large mixer bowl combine sugar, butter, salt and vanilla. Beat at medium speed, scraping bowl often, until creamy (2 to 3 minutes). Reduce speed to low; add flour. Continue beating until well mixed (2 to 3 minutes). (Mixture will form clumps.) By hand, stir in peanuts and chocolate chips. Press on bottom of 15x10x1-inch jelly roll pan. Bake for 15 to 25 minutes or until edges are golden brown. Cool completely.

In medium bowl stir together powdered sugar and peanut butter. Gradually stir in enough hot water for desired glazing consistency. Drizzle glaze over bars. Cut into bars or break into irregular pieces. **YIELD:** 48 bars.

VARIATION

<u>Almond Bark</u>: <u>Omit peanuts and chocolate chips. Omit peanut butter in glaze.</u> Prepare bars using 1 cup sliced almonds and 1 cup milk chocolate chips. Prepare glaze using 2 tablespoons softened LAND O LAKES® Butter and 1/2 teaspoon almond extract.

Nutrition Information (1 bar): Calories 120; Protein 2g; Carbohydrate 13g; Fat 7g; Cholesterol 10mg; Sodium 90mg

Lemon-Butter Bars

Tangy lemon and creamy butter combine to make these classic bars.

Preparation time: 30 minutes • Baking time: 33 minutes

Crust
1⅓ cups all-purpose flour
¼ cup sugar
½ cup LAND O LAKES®
    Butter, softened

Filling
¾ cup sugar
2 eggs
2 tablespoons all-purpose
    flour
¼ teaspoon baking powder
3 tablespoons lemon juice

Powdered sugar

Heat oven to 350°. In small mixer bowl combine all crust ingredients. Beat at low speed, scraping bowl often, until mixture is crumbly (2 to 3 minutes). Press on bottom of 8-inch square baking pan. Bake for 15 to 20 minutes or until edges are lightly browned.

Meanwhile, in small mixer bowl combine all filling ingredients <u>except</u> powdered sugar. Beat at low speed, scraping bowl often, until well mixed. Pour filling over hot partially baked crust. Continue baking for 18 to 20 minutes or until filling is set. Sprinkle with powdered sugar while still warm and again when cool. Cut into bars. **YIELD:** 16 bars.

Nutrition Information (1 bar): Calories 150; Protein 2g; Carbohydrate 22g; Fat 6g; Cholesterol 40mg; Sodium 70mg

Lemon-Butter Bars; Strawberry Marzipan Bars, see page 76

Strawberry Marzipan Bars

*These European-inspired bars have a very special flavor and texture
that makes them rich and extra elegant!*

*Preparation time: 30 minutes • Baking time: 35 minutes • Cooling time: 30 minutes
(pictured on page 75)*

Crumb Mixture
1¼ cups all-purpose flour
⅓ cup firmly packed brown
   sugar
½ cup LAND O LAKES®
   Butter, softened

Filling
¾ cup strawberry preserves

½ cup all-purpose flour
½ cup firmly packed brown
   sugar
¼ cup LAND O LAKES®
   Butter, softened
½ teaspoon almond extract

Glaze
½ cup powdered sugar
½ teaspoon almond extract
1 to 2 teaspoons milk

Heat oven to 350°. In small mixer bowl combine all crumb mixture ingredients. Beat at low speed, scraping bowl often, until mixture is crumbly (1 to 2 minutes). Press on bottom of greased and floured 8- or 9-inch square baking pan. Bake for 15 to 20 minutes or until edges are lightly browned.

Spread preserves to within ¼ inch of edge. In same mixer bowl combine all remaining filling ingredients. Beat at low speed, scraping bowl often, until well mixed (1 to 2 minutes). Sprinkle filling ingredients over preserves. Continue baking for 20 to 25 minutes or until edges are lightly browned. Cool completely.

In small bowl stir together powdered sugar and ½ teaspoon almond extract. Gradually stir in enough milk for desired drizzling consistency. Drizzle over cooled bars; cut into bars. **YIELD:** 36 bars.

*Nutrition Information (1 bar): Calories 100; Protein 1g; Carbohydrate 15g; Fat 4g;
Cholesterol 10mg; Sodium 40mg*

Grasshopper Butter Cream Bars

A combination of mint and chocolate makes this
butter cream frosted bar taste like a grasshopper pie.

Preparation time: 30 minutes • Baking time: 15 minutes • Cooling time: 20 minutes • Chilling time: 1 hour
(pictured on page 79)

Crust

- 3/4 cup sugar
- 3/4 cup LAND O LAKES® Butter, softened
- 1 tablespoon whipping cream or milk
- 1 1/2 cups all-purpose flour
- 1/2 cup chopped hazelnuts, filberts or walnuts
- 1/2 teaspoon baking powder
- 1/2 teaspoon crème de menthe flavoring*

- 1 (6-ounce) package (1 cup) semi-sweet real chocolate chips

Topping

- 4 cups powdered sugar
- 1/4 cup LAND O LAKES® Butter, softened
- 1 (3-ounce) package cream cheese, softened
- 1/2 teaspoon salt
- 1/2 teaspoon crème de menthe flavoring*
- 3 to 4 tablespoons whipping cream or milk

Heat oven to 350°. In small mixer bowl combine sugar, 3/4 cup butter and 1 tablespoon cream. Beat at medium speed, scraping bowl often, until creamy (1 minute). By hand, stir in all remaining crust ingredients except chocolate chips. Press on bottom of 13x9-inch baking pan. Bake for 15 to 20 minutes or until edges are lightly browned. Sprinkle with chocolate chips. Let stand 2 minutes; spread chips over crust. Cool 20 minutes.

Meanwhile, in large mixer bowl combine powdered sugar, 1/4 cup butter, cream cheese, salt and 1/2 teaspoon crème de menthe flavoring. Beat at medium speed, scraping bowl often and gradually adding enough whipping cream for desired spreading consistency. Spread over cooled chocolate layer. Cover; refrigerate until firm (at least 1 hour). Cut into bars. Store refrigerated. **YIELD:** 48 bars.

* 1/2 teaspoon peppermint extract can be substituted for 1/2 teaspoon crème de menthe flavoring.

Nutrition Information (1 bar): Calories 130; Protein 1g; Carbohydrate 17g; Fat 7g; Cholesterol 15mg; Sodium 70mg

Old-World Raspberry Bars

Rich, moist bars filled with flavorful raspberry preserves.

Preparation time: 15 minutes • Baking time: 40 minutes
(pictured on page 67)

2¼ cups all-purpose flour
  1 cup sugar
  1 cup chopped pecans
  1 cup LAND O LAKES®
      Butter, softened
  1 egg

  1 (10-ounce) jar (¾ cup)
      raspberry preserves*

Heat oven to 350°. In large mixer bowl combine all ingredients <u>except</u> raspberry preserves. Beat at low speed, scraping bowl often, until well mixed (2 to 3 minutes). <u>Reserve 1½ cups mixture</u>; set aside. Press remaining mixture on bottom of greased 8-inch square baking pan. Spread preserves to within ½ inch of edge. Crumble reserved mixture over preserves. Bake for 40 to 50 minutes or until lightly browned. Cool completely; cut into bars. **YIELD:** 25 bars.

*1 (10-ounce) jar of your favorite flavor preserves can be substituted for 1 (10-ounce) jar raspberry preserves.

Nutrition Information (1 bar): Calories 210; Protein 2g; Carbohydrate 27g; Fat 11g; Cholesterol 30mg; Sodium 85mg

Old-World Raspberry Bars; Grasshopper Butter Cream Bars, see page 77

Fruit-Filled White Chocolate Brownies

Apricots, cranberries and raisins fill these white chocolate brownies.

Preparation time: 45 minutes • Baking time: 40 minutes
(pictured on page 83)

½ cup LAND O LAKES® Butter

1 (12-ounce) package (2 cups)
   vanilla milk chips*

2 eggs

¼ cup sugar

1¼ cups all-purpose flour

⅓ cup orange juice

½ teaspoon salt

⅓ cup chopped dried apricots

⅓ cup chopped cranberries

¼ cup golden raisins

2 tablespoons firmly packed
   brown sugar

⅓ cup chopped walnuts,
   toasted

Heat oven to 325°. In 1-quart saucepan melt butter. Remove from heat. Add 1 cup vanilla milk chips; do not stir. Set aside.

In large mixer bowl beat eggs at medium speed until foamy (1 to 2 minutes). Increase speed to high; add sugar. Beat, scraping bowl often, until thick and lemon colored (2 to 3 minutes). Reduce speed to low; add reserved butter and vanilla chip mixture, flour, orange juice and salt. Continue beating, scraping bowl often, until just combined (1 minute). Spread half of batter (about 1¼ cups) into greased and floured 9-inch square baking pan. Bake for 15 to 18 minutes or until edges are light golden brown.

Sprinkle apricots, cranberries, raisins and brown sugar over hot partially baked brownies. Stir remaining 1 cup vanilla milk chips into remaining batter; spread over fruit. (Some fruit may show through batter.) Sprinkle with walnuts. Bake for 25 to 35 minutes or until edges are light golden brown. Cool completely; cut into bars.

YIELD: 25 brownies.

* 12 ounces white chocolate, chopped, can be substituted for 1 (12-ounce) package (2 cups) vanilla milk chips.

Nutrition Information (1 brownie): Calories 170; Protein 3g; Carbohydrate 19g; Fat 10g; Cholesterol 25mg; Sodium 110mg

Crazy-Topped Brownies

***An all-time favorite jazzed up with peanut butter
frosting and toppings of your choice.***

Preparation time: 35 minutes • Baking time: 20 minutes • Cooling time: 30 minutes

Brownies
  1/2 cup LAND O LAKES®
      Butter
  2 (1-ounce) squares
      unsweetened baking
      chocolate
  1 cup sugar
  3/4 cup all-purpose flour
  2 eggs

Frosting
  1 cup powdered sugar
  1/3 cup peanut butter
  1 1/2 teaspoons vanilla
  2 to 3 tablespoons milk

Toppings
      Semi-sweet chocolate
      chips, raisins, salted
      peanuts, etc.

Heat oven to 350°. In 2-quart saucepan melt butter and unsweetened chocolate over medium heat, stirring constantly, until smooth (4 to 6 minutes). Stir in sugar, flour and eggs until well mixed. Spread into greased 8- or 9-inch square baking pan. Bake for 20 to 25 minutes or until brownie begins to pull away from sides of pan. DO NOT OVERBAKE. Cool completely.

In small mixer bowl combine all frosting ingredients <u>except</u> milk. Beat at medium speed, gradually adding enough milk for desired spreading consistency. Spread over cooled brownies.

Sprinkle with any combination of desired toppings (about 1 cup total); press lightly into frosting. Cut into bars. **YIELD:** 25 brownies.

Nutrition Information (1 brownie without topping): Calories 160; Protein 2g; Carbohydrate 20g; Fat 10g; Cholesterol 26mg; Sodium 60mg

Irish Mist Brownies

*A fudgy brownie, layered with mint butter
cream and drizzled with chocolate.*

Preparation time: 30 minutes • Baking time: 25 minutes • Cooling time: 30 minutes

Brownies

1/2 cup LAND O LAKES® Butter

2 (1-ounce) squares
   unsweetened baking
   chocolate

1 cup sugar

3/4 cup all-purpose flour

2 eggs

Filling

2 cups powdered sugar

1 (3-ounce) package cream
   cheese, softened

3 tablespoons
   LAND O LAKES® Butter,
   softened

1/2 teaspoon peppermint
   extract

5 drops green food coloring

2 drops yellow food coloring

1/2 cup real semi-sweet
   chocolate chips, melted

Heat oven to 350°. In 2-quart saucepan melt 1/2 cup butter and 2 squares chocolate over medium heat, stirring constantly, until smooth (4 to 6 minutes). Stir in all remaining brownie ingredients until well mixed. Spread into greased 8- or 9-inch square baking pan. Bake for 25 to 30 minutes or until brownie begins to pull away from sides of pan. Cool completely.

In small mixer bowl combine all filling ingredients <u>except</u> chocolate chips. Beat at medium speed, scraping bowl often, until creamy (2 to 3 minutes). Spread over cooled bars. Drizzle with melted chocolate chips. Cool completely; cut into bars. Store refrigerated.

YIELD: 25 brownies.

Nutrition Information (1 brownie): Calories 160; Protein 2g; Carbohydrate 20g; Fat 9g; Cholesterol 35mg; Sodium 65mg

Nutty Caramel Layer Brownies

Pecans, chocolate and caramels create an all-time favorite brownie.

Preparation time: 30 minutes • Baking time: 35 minutes • Cooling time: 15 minutes

Caramel
$1/3$ cup evaporated milk
1 (14-ounce) package
    caramels, unwrapped

Brownies
$1/2$ cup firmly packed brown
    sugar
$1/2$ cup sugar
1 cup LAND O LAKES®
    Butter, softened
3 eggs
1 (4-ounce) bar sweet cooking
    chocolate, melted
1 teaspoon vanilla
$1^1/2$ cups all-purpose flour
$1/2$ cup chopped pecans

1 ($11^1/2$-ounce) package (2 cups)
    milk chocolate chips
1 cup coarsely chopped pecans

Heat oven to 350°. In 2-quart saucepan combine evaporated milk and caramels. Cook over medium heat, stirring occasionally, until caramels are melted (6 to 8 minutes); set aside.

In large mixer bowl combine brown sugar, sugar and butter. Beat at medium speed, scraping bowl often, until creamy (2 to 3 minutes). Add eggs, chocolate and vanilla. Continue beating, scraping bowl often, until well mixed (1 to 2 minutes). Reduce speed to low; add flour. Continue beating, scraping bowl often, until just combined (1 minute). By hand, stir in $1/2$ cup chopped pecans. Spread $2^1/2$ cups batter into greased 13x9-inch baking pan. Bake 15 minutes.

Sprinkle chocolate chips over hot partially baked brownie; spread caramel mixture over chips. Spoon remaining batter over caramel mixture; spread. (Batter may not cover all of caramel mixture.) Sprinkle 1 cup pecans over batter. Bake for 20 to 30 minutes or until toothpick inserted at angle in top layer of brownie comes out clean. Cool 15 minutes; refrigerate until set. Cut into bars.
YIELD: 36 brownies.

Nutrition Information (1 brownie): Calories 240; Protein 3g; Carbohydrate 27g; Fat 14g; Cholesterol 35mg; Sodium 95mg

Candy & Peanut Brownies

This colorful brownie will tempt you at first sight.

Preparation time: 20 minutes • Baking time: 30 minutes

1/2 cup sugar

1/2 cup firmly packed brown
   sugar

1/2 cup LAND O LAKES®
   Butter, softened

2 eggs

2 (1-ounce) squares
   unsweetened chocolate,
   melted, cooled

1 teaspoon vanilla

1/2 cup all-purpose flour

3/4 cup candy coated milk
   chocolate pieces

1/4 cup salted peanuts

Heat oven to 350°. In large mixer bowl combine sugar, brown sugar and butter. Beat at medium speed, scraping bowl often, until creamy (2 to 3 minutes). Add eggs, unsweetened chocolate and vanilla. Continue beating, scraping bowl often, until well mixed (1 to 2 minutes). Add flour; continue beating, scraping bowl often, just until mixed (1 minute). By hand, stir in 1/2 cup chocolate pieces and peanuts. Spread batter into greased 8-inch square baking pan. Sprinkle remaining 1/4 cup chocolate pieces on batter. Bake for 30 to 40 minutes or until center is set and toothpick inserted in center comes out clean. **YIELD:** 16 brownies.

Nutrition Facts (1 brownie): Calories 200; Protein 3g; Carbohydrate 22g; Fat 12g; Cholesterol 45mg; Sodium 95mg

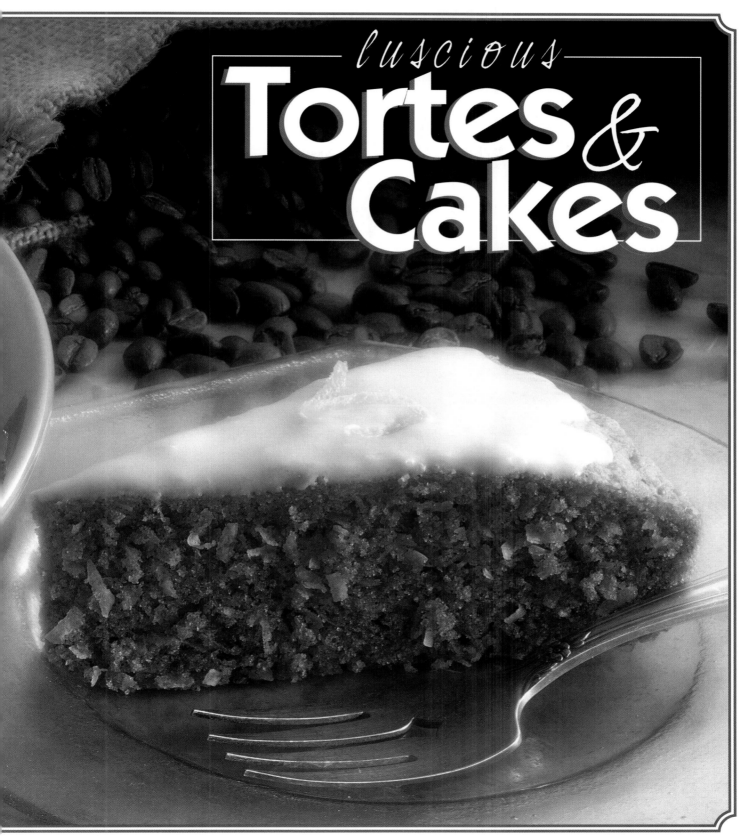

luscious
Tortes & Cakes

Chocolate Mocha Cheesecake and Glazed Carrot Cake Wedges

Chocolate Mocha Cheesecake

*Two favorite flavors, coffee and chocolate, are combined
in this rich and creamy cheesecake.*

Preparation time: 40 minutes • Baking time: 3 hours 20 minutes • Chilling time: 8 hours

Crust

1 1/3 cups graham cracker
crumbs
1/4 cup
LAND O LAKES® Butter,
melted
2 tablespoons sugar

Filling

3/4 cup sugar
1/2 cup LAND O LAKES®
Light Sour Cream
3 (8 ounce) packages cream
cheese, softened
3 tablespoons all-purpose
flour
3 eggs
1 tablespoon vanilla
1 to 2 teaspoons instant
coffee granules
1 tablespoon warm water
1/4 cup sugar
1/4 cup unsweetened cocoa
3 tablespoons
LAND O LAKES® Butter,
melted

Topping

2 (1.4 ounce) chocolate-
coated English toffee bars,
chopped

Heat oven to 325°. In medium bowl stir together all crust
ingredients. Press crumb mixture evenly onto bottom of 9-inch
springform pan. Bake 10 minutes; cool. In large mixer bowl
combine 3/4 cup sugar, Light Sour Cream, cream cheese and flour.
Beat at medium speed, scraping bowl often, until smooth and
creamy (2 to 3 minutes). Add eggs and vanilla. Continue beating,
scraping bowl often, until well-mixed (1 to 2 minutes). In medium
bowl stir together coffee granules and water until granules dissolve.
Add <u>1 cup</u> cream cheese mixture; stir until well mixed. Set aside.
In small bowl combine all remaining filling ingredients; stir until
smooth. Add cocoa mixture to remaining cream cheese mixture;
by hand, stir until well mixed. Pour chocolate cream cheese mixture
into crust. Pour coffee mixture over chocolate mixture. Pull knife
through batter for marbled effect. Bake for 50 to 70 minutes or
until center is set. <u>Turn off oven</u>; leave cheesecake in oven for
2 hours. Loosen sides of cheesecake from pan by running knife
around inside of pan. Cool completely. Sprinkle topping over
cheesecake. Cover; refrigerate 8 hours or overnight. Store
refrigerated. **YIELD:** 12 servings.

*Nutrition Information (1 serving): Calories 440; Protein 8g; Carbohydrate 35g; Fat 32g;
Cholesterol 136mg; Sodium 360mg.*

Glazed Carrot Cake Wedges

No one can resist a wedge of this rich carrot cake with an orange cream cheese glaze.

Preparation time: 30 minutes • Baking time: 40 minutes

Cake

- 1 1/2 cups all-purpose flour
- 1 cup sugar
- 1 1/2 teaspoons baking soda
- 1 teaspoon cinnamon
- 1/2 teaspoon salt
- 3/4 cup vegetable oil
- 2 eggs, slightly beaten
- 1 teaspoon vanilla
- 3 medium (1 1/2 cups) carrots, finely shredded
- 1 cup flaked coconut

Glaze

- 1 cup powdered sugar
- 1 (3-ounce) package cream cheese, softened
- 1 tablespoon grated orange peel
- 1 tablespoon orange juice

Heat oven to 350°. In large bowl combine flour, sugar, baking soda, cinnamon and salt. Stir in oil, eggs and vanilla until well mixed. Gently stir in carrots and coconut. (Batter will be thick.) Spread into greased and floured 9-inch round cake pan. Bake for 40 to 45 minutes or until toothpick inserted in center comes out clean.

Meanwhile, in small mixer bowl combine all glaze ingredients. Beat at low speed, scraping bowl often, until smooth (1 minute). Pour over warm cake. Cut into wedges. **YIELD:** 10 servings.

Nutrition Facts (1 serving): Calories 420; Protein 4g; Carbohydrate 50g; Fat 23g; Cholesterol 50mg; Sodium 320mg

Chocolate Mint Layered Torte

This elegant four-layer torte can be made with either chocolate-mint or mocha filling.

Preparation time: 1 hour 30 minutes • Baking time: 25 minutes • Cooling time: 40 minutes • Chilling time: 1 hour

Cake

2 cups all-purpose flour
1 1/2 cups sugar
1/2 cup unsweetened cocoa
1/2 cup
   LAND O LAKES® Butter,
   softened
1 cup water
3 eggs
1 1/4 teaspoons baking powder
1 teaspoon baking soda
1 teaspoon vanilla

Filling

2 cups (1 pint) whipping cream
1 1/2 teaspoons mint extract
2 tablespoons sugar

Glaze

2 tablespoons
   LAND O LAKES® Butter
1/2 cup semi-sweet real
   chocolate chips
2 tablespoons light corn syrup
1/4 teaspoon mint extract

Heat oven to 350°. Grease 2 (9-inch) round cake pans. Line each pan with 9-inch round piece of waxed paper; grease waxed paper. Set aside. In large mixer bowl combine all cake ingredients. Beat at medium speed, scraping bowl often, until smooth (2 to 3 minutes). Pour batter into prepared pans. Bake for 20 to 25 minutes or until wooden pick inserted in center comes out clean. Cool 10 minutes; remove from pans. Remove waxed paper; cool completely. In chilled small mixer bowl combine chilled whipping cream and 1 1/2 teaspoons mint extract. Beat at high speed, scraping bowl often, until soft peaks form. Continue beating, gradually adding sugar, until stiff peaks form (1 to 2 minutes). Reserve 1/2 cup filling for garnish; refrigerate.

Using serrated knife, cut each cake layer horizontally in half. To assemble torte, place one split cake layer on serving plate; spread with 1/3 filling. Repeat with remaining cake layers and filling, ending with cake layer. Refrigerate torte at least 1 hour. In 1-quart saucepan melt 2 tablespoons butter. Stir in chocolate chips and corn syrup. Cook over low heat, stirring constantly, until chocolate chips are melted (2 to 3 minutes). Remove from heat; stir in 1/4 teaspoon mint extract. Spread glaze over top of torte, allowing glaze to drizzle down sides. Garnish with reserved 1/2 cup filling. Refrigerate until ready to serve. **YIELD:** 16 servings.

VARIATION

Chocolate Mocha Torte: Omit 1 1/2 teaspoons mint extract in filling and 1/4 teaspoon mint extract in glaze. Add 3 tablespoons coffee-flavored liqueur to filling and 1 teaspoon coffee-flavored liqueur to glaze.

Nutrition Information (1 serving): Calories 480; Protein 6g; Carbohydrate 52g; Fat 29g; Cholesterol 150mg; Sodium 287mg.

Tiramisu Torte

Tira mi su is Italian for "pick me up." We've created a luscious torte using the flavors of this popular dessert.

Preparation time: 1 hour • Baking time: 14 minutes • Cooling time: 1 hour • Chilling time: 3 hours

Cake

- 4 eggs, separated
- 3/4 cup sugar
- 3 tablespoons water
- 1/2 teaspoon vanilla
- 3/4 cup all-purpose flour
- 1 teaspoon baking powder

Syrup

- 1/2 cup sugar
- 1/2 cup water
- 2 tablespoons instant espresso powder
- 2 tablespoons dark rum*

Filling

- 1/2 cup powdered sugar
- 2 (8-ounce) containers mascarpone cheese **or** cream cheese
- 1/2 teaspoon vanilla
- 3 (1-ounce) squares semi-sweet baking chocolate, grated

Frosting

- 1 pint (2 cups) whipping cream

   Chocolate covered coffee beans, if desired

Heat oven to 375°. Grease 15x10x1-inch jelly roll pan. Line with waxed paper; grease paper. In large mixer bowl beat egg whites at high speed until foamy (1 to 2 minutes). Continue beating, gradually adding 1/4 cup sugar, until glossy and stiff peaks form (2 to 3 minutes). In small mixer bowl combine remaining 1/2 cup sugar, egg yolks, 3 tablespoons water and 1/2 teaspoon vanilla. Beat at high speed, scraping bowl often, until thick and light (5 to 6 minutes). By hand, gently stir in flour and baking powder. Gently stir egg yolk mixture into beaten egg whites. Pour into prepared pan. Bake for 14 to 18 minutes or until top springs back when touched lightly in center. Cool 10 minutes; remove from pan. Cool completely.

In 1-quart saucepan combine 1/2 cup sugar, 1/2 cup water and espresso powder. Cook over medium heat until mixture comes to a full boil (3 to 4 minutes). Boil 1 minute; stir in rum. Cool completely. Cut cake crosswise into 3 (10x5-inch) pieces. Brush each piece generously with syrup reserving 2 tablespoons syrup.

Place 1 piece of cake on serving plate. In medium bowl stir together powdered sugar, mascarpone cheese and vanilla. Stir in 2 ounces grated chocolate. Spread half of filling on top of cake on serving plate. Repeat layering; top with third cake layer.

In chilled larger mixer bowl beat chilled whipping cream at high speed until soft peaks form (1 to 2 minutes). Continue beating, gradually adding 2 tablespoons syrup until stiff peaks form (2 to 3 minutes). Spread 1 cup whipped cream on top of cake; sprinkle with remaining grated chocolate. Pipe or spread remaining whipped cream on sides of cake. Garnish with chocolate covered coffee beans. Refrigerate at least 3 hours. To serve, cut torte into 8 slices; cut each slice in half. Store refrigerated. **YIELD: 16 servings.**

*1 teaspoon rum extract can be substituted for 2 tablespoons dark rum.

Nutrition Facts (1 serving): Calories 350; Protein 5g; Carbohydrate 28g; Fat 24g; Cholesterol 125mg; Sodium 130mg

Blueberry-Peach Ice Cream Torte

Fresh peaches swirled in ice cream and topped with a blueberry sauce make an elegant presentation.

Preparation time: 1 hour • Freezing time: 12 hours

2 cups (3 medium) fresh
   peaches, peeled, sliced*
2 tablespoons sugar
1 package (12) ladyfingers,
   split
1/2 gallon vanilla ice cream,
   slightly softened

Sauce
1/3 cup sugar
2 tablespoons cornstarch
1 cup water
2 tablespoons
   LAND O LAKES® Butter
2 tablespoons lemon juice
1 teaspoon grated lemon peel
2 cups fresh <u>or</u> frozen blueberries (do not thaw)

In 5-cup blender container combine peach slices and 2 tablespoons sugar. Cover; blend at High speed until well blended (30 to 40 seconds). Set aside. Place split ladyfingers upright (rounded side out) around edge of 10-inch springform pan, fitting closely together. Place ice cream in large bowl. Swirl in peach mixture. Place, by spoonfuls, evenly into prepared pan, pressing gently to level ice cream. Cover with aluminum foil; freeze at least 12 hours or overnight. In 2-quart saucepan combine 1/3 cup sugar and cornstarch; stir in water. Cook over medium heat, stirring occasionally, until mixture thickens and comes to a full boil (3 to 5 minutes). Boil 1 minute. Stir in butter, lemon juice and lemon peel. Cool 10 minutes. Stir in blueberries. Just before serving, pour sauce over top of torte. **YIELD:** 12 servings.

*2 cups frozen sliced peaches, thawed, can be substituted for 2 cups fresh peaches.

TIP: 9-inch round cake pan can be substituted for 10-inch springform pan. Line with aluminum foil, extending excess aluminum foil over edges. After torte is frozen, lift torte from pan, using aluminum foil as handles. Remove aluminum foil.

TIP: Fresh blueberries make a clear sauce; frozen blueberries make a blueberry-colored sauce.

Nutrition Information (1 serving): Calories 300; Protein 4g; Carbohydrate 44g; Fat 12g; Cholesterol 84mg; Sodium 105mg.

Raspberry Crowned Chocolate Torte

A rich brownie-like torte is topped with glistening raspberry preserves and garnished with whipped cream.

Preparation time: 1 hour • Baking time: 55 minutes • Cooling time: 1 hour • Chilling time: 3 hours

3 eggs, separated
1/8 teaspoon cream of tartar
1/8 teaspoon salt
1 1/2 cups sugar
1 cup
   LAND O LAKES® Butter,
   melted
1 1/2 teaspoons vanilla
1/2 cup all-purpose flour
1/2 cup unsweetened cocoa
3 tablespoons water
3/4 cup finely chopped
   almonds

1/3 cup raspberry preserves

Sweetened whipped cream
Fresh raspberries

Heat oven to 350°. Grease 9-inch round cake pan. Line with aluminum foil, leaving excess foil over edges; grease foil. Set aside. In small mixer bowl combine egg whites, cream of tartar and salt. Beat at high speed, scraping bowl often, until soft peaks form (1 to 2 minutes); set aside. In large mixer bowl combine egg yolks, sugar, butter and vanilla. Beat at medium speed, scaping bowl often, until well mixed (1 to 2 minutes). Add flour, cocoa and water. Continue beating, scraping bowl often, until well mixed (1 to 2 minutes). Stir in chopped almonds. Fold beaten egg whites into chocolate mixture. Spread into prepared pan. Bake for 40 to 55 minutes or until firm to the touch. (Do not overbake.) Cool on wire rack 1 hour; remove from pan by lifting aluminum foil. Cover; refrigerate until completely cooled (2 to 3 hours). Remove aluminum foil; place on serving plate. Spread raspberry preserves on top. Garnish with sweetened whipped cream and raspberries. **YIELD:** 12 servings.

Nutrition Information (1 serving): Calories 350; Protein 5g; Carbohydrate 38g; Fat 22g; Cholesterol 111mg; Sodium 226mg.

Special Occasion Layer Cake

*Creme de cacao, chocolate butter cream and white chocolate frosting
combine to make this three-tier cake perfect for special occasions.*

Preparation time: 1 hour • Baking time: 25 minutes • Cooling time: 35 minutes

Cake

2 cups all-purpose flour

1 1/2 cups sugar

1/2 cup
LAND O LAKES® Butter,
softened

1 cup milk

4 egg whites

3 1/2 teaspoons baking powder

1/2 teaspoon salt

1 teaspoon vanilla

6 tablespoons creme de cacao

Filling

1/2 cup powdered sugar

1/4 cup
LAND O LAKES® Butter,
softened

1 (1 ounce) square unsweetened baking chocolate,
melted, cooled

1 tablespoon whipping cream

Frosting

2 cups powdered sugar

1/4 cup
LAND O LAKES® Butter,
softened

3 ounces white chocolate,
melted, cooled

4 to 5 tablespoons whipping
cream

White & dark chocolate leaves

Heat oven to 350°. In large mixer bowl combine all cake ingredients <u>except</u> creme de cacao. Beat at low speed, scraping bowl often, until all ingredients are moistened. Beat at high speed, scraping bowl often, until smooth (3 to 4 minutes). Pour into 3 greased and floured 8-inch round cake pans. Bake for 20 to 25 minutes or until wooden pick inserted in center comes out clean. Cool 5 minutes; remove from pans. Cool completely. In small mixer bowl combine all filling ingredients. Beat at high speed, scraping bowl often, until light and fluffy (2 to 3 minutes); set aside. In small mixer bowl combine all frosting ingredients. Beat at high speed, scraping bowl often, until light and fluffy (2 to 3 minutes). To assemble cake, place 1 layer on serving plate. Poke top of cake all over with fork; sprinkle with <u>2 tablespoons</u> creme de cacao. Spread with <u>1/2</u> filling. Place second cake layer on top. Poke top of cake all over with fork; sprinkle with <u>2 tablespoons</u> creme de cacao. Spread with remaining filling. Place third cake layer on top. Poke top of cake all over with fork; sprinkle with <u>2 tablespoons</u> creme de cacao. Frost entire cake with frosting. If desired, garnish with chocolate leaves. **YIELD:** 12 servings.

TIP: 3 (9-inch) round cake pans can be substituted for 3 (8-inch) round cake pans. Bake for 15 to 20 minutes or until wooden pick inserted in center comes out clean.

Nutrition Information (1 serving): Calories 510; Protein 5g; Carbohydrate 75g; Fat 22g; Cholesterol 54mg; Sodium 374mg.

Chocolate Sponge Cake with Fresh Fruit

This unique mixture of chocolate and fruit is perfect for any season.

Preparation time: 45 minutes • Baking time: 23 minutes • Cooling time: 30 minutes

Cake

1 cup powdered sugar

4 eggs, room temperature

1 egg yolk, room temperature

1 tablespoon creme de cacao*

1/2 cup all-purpose flour

1/4 cup Dutch process cocoa <u>or</u> unsweetened cocoa

1/8 teaspoon salt

2 tablespoons LAND O LAKES® Butter, melted

Topping

1 pint strawberries, hulled, cut in half

1 kiwi, peeled, sliced 1/8-inch, cut in half

1/2 cup fresh raspberries

1/2 cup fresh blueberries

1 cup apple jelly, heated until liquid

Sweetened whipped cream

Heat oven to 375°. Grease and flour 10-inch removable-bottom tart pan. Place pan on cookie sheet; set aside. In large mixer bowl combine powdered sugar, eggs, egg yolk and creme de cacao. Beat at high speed, scraping bowl often, until mixture is very thick and double in volume (5 to 8 minutes). (Mixture should be light yellow and consistency of soft whipped cream.) In medium bowl sift together flour, cocoa and salt. By hand, gently fold flour mixture into egg mixture just until flour is moistened. Fold butter into batter. Gently spoon batter into prepared pan. Bake for 20 to 23 minutes or until wooden pick inserted in center comes out clean. Cool completely on wire rack. To serve, decoratively arrange fresh fruit on top of cake. Drizzle warm jelly over top of cake and fruit. Garnish with sweetened whipped cream. **YIELD:** 12 servings.

*1 teaspoon vanilla can be substituted for 1 tablespoon creme de cacao.

Nutrition Information (1 serving): Calories 190; Protein 4g; Carbohydrate 35g; Fat 5g; Cholesterol 95mg; Sodium 80mg.

Lemon Poppy Seed Pound Cake

**Lemon complements the rich, moist flavor of
this delicate cake.**

Preparation time: 30 minutes • Baking time: 65 minutes • Cooling time: 1 hour 30 minutes

Cake

3 cups all-purpose flour

2 cups sugar

1/4 cup poppy seed

1 cup
   LAND O LAKES® Butter,
   softened

1 cup buttermilk*

4 eggs

1/2 teaspoon baking soda

1/2 teaspoon baking powder

1/2 teaspoon salt

4 teaspoons grated lemon peel

1/2 teaspoon vanilla

Glaze

1 cup powdered sugar

1 to 2 tablespoons lemon juice

Heat oven to 325°. In large mixer bowl combine all cake ingredients. Beat at low speed, scraping bowl often, until all ingredients are moistened. Beat at high speed, scraping bowl often, until smooth (1 to 2 minutes). Pour into greased and floured 12-cup Bundt pan or 10-inch tube pan. Bake for 55 to 65 minutes or until wooden pick inserted in center comes out clean. Cool 10 minutes; remove from pan. Cool completely. In small bowl stir together powdered sugar and lemon juice until smooth. Drizzle over cake. **YIELD:** 16 servings.

*1 tablespoon vinegar plus enough milk to equal 1 cup can be substituted
  for 1 cup buttermilk.

*Nutrition Information (1 serving): Calories 340; Protein 5g; Carbohydrate 51g; Fat 14g;
Cholesterol 85mg; Sodium 260mg.*

Chocolate Rocky Road Cake

**Chocolate, marshmallows and peanuts
top this moist chocolate cake.**

Preparation time: 45 minutes • Baking time: 42 minutes

Cake

2 cups all-purpose flour

1 1/2 cups sugar

1/2 cup unsweetened cocoa

1/2 cup
  LAND O LAKES® Butter,
  softened

1 cup water

3 eggs

1 1/4 teaspoons baking powder

1 teaspoon baking soda

1 teaspoon vanilla

Frosting

2 cups miniature
  marshmallows

1/4 cup
  LAND O LAKES® Butter

1 (3 ounce) package cream
  cheese

1 (1 ounce) square unsweetened
  baking chocolate

2 tablespoons milk

3 cups powdered sugar

1 teaspoon vanilla

1/2 cup coarsely chopped
  salted peanuts

Heat oven to 350°. In large mixer bowl combine all cake ingredients. Beat at low speed, scraping bowl often, until ingredients are moistened. Beat at high speed, scraping bowl often, until smooth (1 to 2 minutes). Pour into greased and floured 13x9-inch baking pan. Bake for 30 to 40 minutes or until wooden pick inserted in center comes out clean. Sprinkle with marshmallows. Continue baking 2 minutes or until marshmallows are softened. Meanwhile, in 2-quart saucepan combine 1/4 cup butter, cream cheese, chocolate and milk. Cook over medium heat, stirring occasionally, until melted (8 to 10 minutes). Remove from heat; stir in powdered sugar and vanilla until smooth. Pour over marshmallows and swirl together. Sprinkle with peanuts.
YIELD: 15 servings.

Nutrition Information (1 serving): Calories 400; Protein 6g; Carbohydrate 61g; Fat 16g; Cholesterol 75mg; Sodium 290mg.

Honey Spice Cake with Orange Cream

A light and creamy orange topping adds a delightful touch to a homemade spice cake.

Preparation time: 45 minutes • Baking time: 40 minutes

Cake

1/2 cup firmly packed brown sugar

1/4 cup LAND O LAKES® Butter, softened

1/3 cup LAND O LAKES® Light Sour Cream

1/3 cup orange juice

1/4 cup honey

2 egg whites

2 cups all-purpose flour

1 teaspoon baking soda

1 teaspoon cinnamon

1/2 teaspoon ginger

1/4 teaspoon salt

Orange Cream

2/3 cup LAND O LAKES® Light Sour Cream

1 tablespoon sugar

1 teaspoon grated orange peel

1 tablespoon orange juice

Heat oven to 325°. In large mixer bowl combine brown sugar, butter, 1/3 cup sour cream, 1/3 cup orange juice, honey and egg whites. Beat at low speed, scraping bowl often, until well mixed (1 to 2 minutes). Continue beating, gradually adding all remaining cake ingredients, until well mixed (1 to 2 minutes). Pour into greased 9-inch round cake pan. Bake for 35 to 40 minutes or until wooden pick inserted in center comes out clean. Meanwhile, in small bowl stir together all orange cream ingredients. Serve cake warm or cool with dolop of orange cream. **YIELD:** 10 servings.

Nutrition Information (1 serving): Calories 240; Protein 4g; Carbohydrate 42g; Fat 6g; Cholesterol 18mg; Sodium 250mg.

Buttery Coconut Pecan Cake

**This moist cake is topped with an old-fashioned
browned butter frosting.**

Preparation time: 30 minutes • Baking time: 45 minutes • Cooling time: 1 hour

Cake
2 1/4 cups all-purpose flour

1 1/2 cups sugar

1 cup
   LAND O LAKES® Butter,
   softened

1 cup buttermilk*

4 eggs

1 teaspoon baking soda

1/2 teaspoon salt

1 tablespoon vanilla

1 cup flaked coconut

1 cup chopped pecans

Frosting
1/3 cup
   LAND O LAKES® Butter

3 cups powdered sugar

1 1/2 teaspoons vanilla

1 to 3 tablespoons milk

Heat oven to 350°. In large mixer bowl combine all cake ingredients <u>except</u> coconut and pecans. Beat at low speed, scraping bowl often, until all ingredients are moistened. Beat at high speed, scraping bowl often, until smooth (3 to 4 minutes). By hand, stir in coconut and pecans. Pour into greased and floured 13x9-inch baking pan. Bake for 45 to 50 minutes or until center of cake is firm to the touch and edges begin to pull away from sides of pan. Cool completely. In 1-quart saucepan heat 1/3 cup butter over medium heat, stirring constantly, until delicate brown (5 to 6 minutes). In small mixer bowl combine melted butter, powdered sugar and vanilla. Beat at medium speed, gradually adding milk and scraping bowl often, until frosting is smooth and spreadable. Frost cooled cake.
YIELD: 15 servings.

*1 tablespoon vinegar plus enough milk to equal 1 cup can be substituted for 1 cup buttermilk.

Nutrition Information (1 serving): Calories 480; Protein 5g; Carbohydrate 63g; Fat 25g; Cholesterol 100mg; Sodium 420mg.

Apricot Pecan Upside-Down Cake

Apricots, pecans and nutmeg help form this delicious "topping" in this upside-down cake.

Preparation time: 30 minutes • Baking time: 30 minutes

Topping

1/2 cup firmly packed brown sugar

1/4 cup LAND O LAKES® Butter

1/4 teaspoon ground nutmeg

1/2 cup chopped pecans

1 (15.25-ounce) can apricot halves, well drained

Cake

2/3 cup firmly packed brown sugar

1/3 cup LAND O LAKES® Butter, softened

2 eggs

3/4 teaspoon grated lemon peel

1 1/2 teaspoons vanilla

1 1/2 cups all-purpose flour

2 teaspoons baking powder

1/4 teaspoon salt

1/2 cup milk

Heat oven to 375°. Cut piece of waxed paper to fit bottom of 9-inch square or 11x7-inch baking pan; place on bottom. In small bowl combine all topping ingredients <u>except</u> pecans and apricots. Stir in pecans. Sprinkle on top of waxed paper. Place apricot halves, rounded side down, on top of brown sugar mixture; set aside.

In large mixer bowl combine $2/3$ cup brown sugar and $1/3$ cup butter. Beat at medium speed, scraping bowl often, until creamy (1 to 2 minutes). Continue beating, adding eggs 1 at a time, until well mixed (1 to 2 minutes). Add lemon peel and vanilla; continue beating until well mixed (1 minute). Reduce speed to low. Beat, gradually adding flour, baking powder and salt alternately with milk and scraping bowl often, until well mixed (1 to 2 minutes). Gently spread batter on top of apricots. Bake for 30 to 40 minutes or until toothpick inserted in center comes out clean. Loosen sides of cake from pan by running a knife around inside of pan. Invert cake onto serving platter; let stand 5 minutes. Remove pan. Gently peel off waxed paper; cool completely.
YIELD: 9 servings.

Nutrition Facts (1 serving): Calories 370; Protein 5g; Carbohydrate 49g; Fat 18g; Cholesterol 80mg; Sodium 280mg

Choco-Scotch Cake

The topping is baked right on the cake in this easy and "toteable" picnic pleaser cake.

Preparation time: 20 minutes • Baking time: 40 minutes

2¹/₂ cups all-purpose flour

1¹/₂ cups sugar

³/₄ cup LAND O LAKES®
Butter, softened

1¹/₄ cups cold water

3 eggs

2 (1-ounce) squares
unsweetened baking
chocolate, melted

1 teaspoon baking soda

1 teaspoon salt

1 teaspoon vanilla

1 cup butterscotch-flavored
chips

¹/₂ cup chopped walnuts

Heat oven to 350°. In large mixer bowl combine all ingredients <u>except</u> butterscotch chips and walnuts. Beat at low speed until moistened. Increase speed to medium. Beat, scraping bowl often, until well mixed (2 minutes). Spread batter into greased 13x9-inch baking pan. Sprinkle with butterscotch chips and walnuts. Bake for 40 to 45 minutes or until top springs back when touched lightly in center. Cool completely.
YIELD: 20 servings.

*Nutrition Facts (1 serving): Calories 260; Protein 4g; Carbohydrate 34g; Fat 14g;
Cholesterol 50mg; Sodium 250mg*

Choco-Swirl Sour Cream Cake

A moist yellow cake is swirled with a rich, hot fudge.

Preparation time: 45 minutes • Baking time: 40 minutes • Cooling time: 1 hour

Cake

2 1/3 cups all-purpose flour
1 1/2 cups sugar
1 teaspoon baking soda
1 teaspoon salt
1/2 teaspoon baking powder
1 cup LAND O LAKES®
   Sour Cream
1/2 cup
   LAND O LAKES® Butter,
   softened
3/4 cup milk
2 eggs
1 teaspoon vanilla
1/2 cup hot fudge topping

Frosting

12 ounces (2 cups) real milk
   chocolate chips
1 cup LAND O LAKES®
   Sour Cream
1/2 teaspoon vanilla

Heat oven to 350°. In large mixer bowl combine all cake ingredients <u>except</u> hot fudge topping. Beat at medium speed, scraping bowl often, until well mixed (2 to 3 minutes). <u>Reserve $^1/_2$ cup cake batter</u>; set aside.

Spread remaining batter into greased 13x9-inch baking pan. In small bowl stir together reserved $^1/_2$ cup cake batter and $^1/_2$ cup hot fudge topping. Drop mixture by spoonfuls evenly over batter. Pull knife through batter for marbled effect. Bake for 40 to 50 minutes or until top springs back when touched lightly in center. Cool completely.

In 1-quart saucepan melt milk chocolate chips over medium heat, stirring constantly, until smooth (2 to 3 minutes). Place melted chocolate in small mixer bowl. Add 1 cup sour cream and $^1/_2$ teaspoon vanilla. Beat at medium speed, scraping bowl often, until smooth and creamy (1 to 2 minutes). Frost cooled cake. **YIELD:** 15 servings.

Nutrition Facts (1 serving): Calories 410; Protein 7g; Carbohydrate 58g; Fat 18g; Cholesterol 60mg; Sodium 360mg

Chocolate Cream Filled Cake

*A creamy filling and a white and dark chocolate glaze makes
this an especially attractive dessert.*

Preparation time: 30 minutes • Baking time: 50 minutes • Cooling time: 1 hour 30 minutes

Filling
- 1/4 cup sugar
- 1 (8-ounce) package cream cheese, softened
- 1 egg
- 1 teaspoon vanilla

Cake
- 2 cups all-purpose flour
- 1 1/2 cups sugar
- 1/2 cup unsweetened cocoa
- 1/2 cup LAND O LAKES® Butter, softened
- 1 cup water
- 3 eggs
- 1 1/4 teaspoons baking powder
- 1 teaspoon baking soda
- 1 teaspoon vanilla

Glaze
- 2 ounces white chocolate
- 2 teaspoons shortening
- 1/4 cup semi-sweet real chocolate chips

Heat oven to 350°. In small mixer bowl combine all filling ingredients. Beat at low speed, scraping bowl often, until smooth (2 to 3 minutes); set aside.

In large mixer bowl combine all cake ingredients. Beat at low speed, scraping bowl often, until all ingredients are moistened. Beat at high speed, scraping bowl often, until smooth (2 to 3 minutes). Pour 3 cups batter into greased and floured 12-cup Bundt pan. Spoon filling over batter without touching sides of pan; cover with remaining batter. Bake for 50 to 60 minutes or until toothpick inserted in center comes out clean. Cool in pan 30 minutes. Remove from pan; cool completely.

In 1-quart saucepan melt white chocolate and 1 teaspoon shortening over low heat, stirring constantly, until melted (1 to 2 minutes). Drizzle over cake. Let stand until firm. Repeat with remaining shortening and chocolate chips. Store refrigerated. **YIELD:** 16 servings.

Nutrition Facts (1 serving): Calories 300; Protein 5g; Carbohydrate 39g; Fat 15g; Cholesterol 85mg; Sodium 230mg

Lemon Picnic Cake with Berries

An old-fashioned butter cake, served with fresh berries, is the perfect dessert for a picnic or potluck.

Preparation time: 30 minutes • Baking time: 50 minutes • Cooling time: 15 minutes

Cake

- 4 eggs, separated
- 2 cups sugar
- 1 cup LAND O LAKES® Butter, softened
- 3 cups all-purpose flour
- 2 teaspoons baking powder
- 1 cup milk
- 2 teaspoons grated lemon peel
- 1 tablespoon lemon juice
- 1 teaspoon vanilla

Glaze

- 1/3 cup sugar
- 1/3 cup lemon juice
- 1 tablespoon grated lemon peel

Fresh berries

Heat oven to 350°. In small mixer bowl beat egg whites at high speed, scraping bowl often, just until stiff peaks form (2 to 3 minutes). Set aside.

In large mixer bowl combine 2 cups sugar and butter. Beat at low speed, scraping bowl often, until creamy (1 to 2 minutes). Add egg yolks; continue beating until creamy (1 to 2 minutes). In small bowl stir together flour and baking powder. Reduce speed to low. Beat, gradually adding flour mixture alternately with milk to butter mixture, until well blended. Add lemon peel, lemon juice and vanilla. Continue beating until well mixed. By hand, gently stir in egg whites. Pour into greased and floured 10-inch tube or 12-cup Bundt pan. Bake for 50 to 65 minutes or until toothpick inserted in center comes out clean.

In 1-quart saucepan stir together all glaze ingredients <u>except</u> berries. Cook over medium heat, stirring occasionally, until sugar is dissolved (3 to 4 minutes). With toothpick poke holes in top of cake; pour glaze over cake. Cool 15 minutes; remove from pan. If desired, leave cake in pan to transport. Serve with fresh berries. **YIELD:** 12 servings.

Nutrition Facts (1 serving): Calories 440; Protein 6g; Carbohydrate 65g; Fat 18g; Cholesterol 115mg; Sodium 240mg

Penuche Frosted Banana Cake

Penuche is a rich creamy frosting made from brown sugar, butter, milk or cream and vanilla.

Preparation time: 30 minutes • Baking time: 40 minutes • Cooling time: 1 hour

Cake

3 1/2 cups all-purpose flour
1 teaspoon baking powder
1 teaspoon baking soda
1/4 teaspoon salt
2 cups sugar
1/2 cup
   LAND O LAKES® Butter, softened
2 eggs
2 medium (1 cup) ripe bananas, mashed
1 cup LAND O LAKES® Sour Cream
1 teaspoon vanilla
1/2 cup chopped walnuts <u>or</u> pecans

Frosting

1/2 cup firmly packed brown sugar
1/4 cup
   LAND O LAKES® Butter
1/3 cup half-and-half
1/8 teaspoon salt
2 1/2 cups powdered sugar
1/2 teaspoon vanilla
1/4 cup chopped walnuts <u>or</u> pecans, if desired

Heat oven to 350°. In medium bowl stir together flour, baking powder, baking soda and $1/4$ teaspoon salt; set aside.

In large mixer bowl combine sugar and $1/2$ cup butter. Beat at medium speed, scraping bowl often, until creamy (2 to 3 minutes). Continue beating, adding eggs 1 at a time, until creamy (1 to 2 minutes). Add bananas, sour cream and vanilla; continue beating until well mixed (1 minute). Continue beating, gradually adding flour mixture and scraping bowl often, until well mixed (1 minute). By hand, stir in $1/2$ cup walnuts. Pour batter into greased 13x9-inch baking pan. Bake for 40 to 50 minutes or until toothpick inserted in center comes out clean. Cool completely.

Meanwhile, in 2-quart saucepan cook brown sugar, $1/4$ cup butter, half-and-half and $1/8$ teaspoon salt over medium heat until mixture comes to a full boil (6 to 8 minutes). Cool to lukewarm (15 to 20 minutes). Stir in all remaining frosting ingredients; beat until smooth. Spread on cooled cake; sprinkle with $1/4$ cup walnuts. **YIELD:** 15 servings.

Nutrition Facts (1 serving): Calories 470; Protein 6g; Carbohydrate 79g; Fat 16g; Cholesterol 60mg; Sodium 70mg

Sweetheart Cheesecake

*Rich homemade cheesecake is sweetened with a
decorative ring of hearts.*

Preparation time: 1 hour • Baking time: 1 hour 30 minutes • Cooling time: 2 hours • Chilling time: 4 hours

Crust

1 1/3 cups crushed chocolate
    wafer cookies

1/3 cup
    LAND O LAKES® Butter,
    melted

2 tablespoons sugar

Filling

4 eggs, separated

1/2 cup
    LAND O LAKES® Butter,
    softened

2 (8 ounce) packages cream
    cheese, softened

1 cup sugar

1 tablespoon cornstarch

1 teaspoon baking powder

1 tablespoon lemon juice

Topping

1 cup LAND O LAKES®
    Light Sour Cream

2 tablespoons sugar

1 teaspoon vanilla

1 (21 ounce) can cherry
    pie filling

3 tablespoons cherry-flavored
    liqueur, if desired

Heat oven to 325°. In small bowl stir together all crust ingredients. Press crumb mixture evenly onto bottom of 9-inch springform pan. Bake 10 minutes; cool. In small mixer bowl beat egg whites at high speed, scraping bowl often, until soft peaks form (1 to 2 minutes); set aside. In large mixer bowl combine 1/2 cup butter, cream cheese and egg yolks. Beat at medium speed, scraping bowl often, until smooth and creamy (2 to 3 minutes). Add all remaining filling ingredients <u>except</u> egg whites. Continue beating, scraping bowl often, until well mixed (1 to 2 minutes). By hand, fold in beaten egg whites. Spoon filling into prepared pan. Bake for 60 to 80 minutes or until center is set and firm to the touch. (Cheesecake surface will be cracked.)

Cool 15 minutes; loosen sides of cheesecake from pan by running knife around inside of pan. Cool completely. (Cheesecake center will dip slightly upon cooling.) In small bowl stir together Light Sour Cream, 2 tablespoons sugar and vanilla. Spread evenly over top of cheesecake. Spoon out 2 to 3 tablespoons of cherry sauce from pie filling; drop by teaspoonfuls onto Light Sour Cream topping. Carefully pull knife or spatula through cherry sauce, forming hearts. Cover; refrigerate 4 hours or overnight. To serve, in medium bowl stir together remaining pie filling and liqueur; spoon over cheese-cake. Store refrigerated. **YIELD:** 12 servings.

*Nutrition Information (1 serving): Calories 490; Protein 7g; Carbohydrate 48g; Fat 29g;
Cholesterol 153mg; Sodium 310mg.*

Cool Key Lime Cheesecake

A cheesecake version of a favorite
Florida dessert.

Preparation time: 30 minutes • Chilling time: 4 hours 45 minutes

Crust
1 cup graham cracker crumbs
1/4 cup sugar
1/3 cup
    LAND O LAKES® Butter,
    melted

Filling
1 cup lime juice
1/4 cup water
2 (1/4 ounce) envelopes
    unflavored gelatin
1 1/2 cups sugar
5 eggs, slightly beaten
1 tablespoon grated lime peel
1/2 cup
    LAND O LAKES® Butter,
    softened
2 (8 ounce) packages cream
    cheese, softened
1/2 cup whipping cream

Sweetened whipped cream
Lime slices

In medium bowl stir together all crust ingredients. Press on bottom of 9-inch springform pan; set aside. In 2-quart saucepan combine lime juice, water and gelatin. Let stand 5 minutes to soften. Add sugar, eggs and lime peel. Cook over medium heat, stirring constantly, until mixture just comes to a boil (7 to 8 minutes). DO NOT BOIL. Set aside. In large mixer bowl combine butter and cream cheese. Beat at medium speed, scraping bowl often, until well mixed (1 to 2 minutes). Continue beating, gradually adding hot lime mixture, until well mixed (1 to 2 minutes). Refrigerate, stirring occasionally, until cool (about 45 minutes). In chilled small mixer bowl beat chilled whipping cream at high speed, scraping bowl often, until stiff peaks form (1 to 2 minutes). Fold into lime mixture. Pour into prepared crust. Cover; refrigerate until firm (3 to 4 hours). Loosen sides of cheesecake from pan by running knife around inside of pan; remove pan. Garnish top of cheesecake with sweetened whipped cream. If desired, garnish with lime slices.
YIELD: 12 servings.

Nutrition Information (1 serving): Calories 460; Protein 7g; Carbohydrate 37g; Fat 33g; Cholesterol 179mg; Sodium 325mg.

Easy Mini-Cheesecakes

Making cheesecake has never been so easy!

Preparation time: 30 minutes • Baking time: 40 minutes • Chilling time: 2 hours

12 foil cupcake liners

12 vanilla wafer cookies
1/2 cup sugar
2 (8 ounce) packages cream
  cheese, softened
2 eggs
1 teaspoon vanilla
1 cup LAND O LAKES®
  Light Sour Cream
2 tablespoons sugar
1 teaspoon vanilla

Chocolate curls
Cut-up fruit
Powdered sugar

Heat oven to 325°. Line 12-cup muffin pan with foil liners; place one cookie in each liner. In large mixer bowl combine 1/2 cup sugar, cream cheese, eggs and vanilla. Beat at medium speed, scraping bowl often, until smooth (2 to 3 minutes). Pour over each cookie, filling cup 3/4 full. Bake for 30 minutes. Meanwhile, in small bowl stir together Light Sour Cream, 2 tablespoons sugar and vanilla. Spoon about 1 tablespoon Light Sour Cream mixture onto each hot cheesecake. Continue baking for 8 to 10 minutes or until set. Cool; remove from pan. Cover; refrigerate until firm (1 to 2 hours). Store refrigerated. To serve, garnish with chocolate curls, fruit and powdered sugar. **YIELD:** 12 servings.

Nutrition Information (1 serving): Calories 250; Protein 5g; Carbohydrate 20g; Fat 17g; Cholesterol 83mg; Sodium 150mg.

Double Chocolate Cheesecake with Raspberry Sauce

Chocolate and white chocolate combine in this heavenly cheesecake topped with raspberry sauce.

Preparation time: 45 minutes • Baking time: 4 hour 25 minutes • Chilling time: 8 hours

Crust

1 1/3 cups graham cracker crumbs

1/4 cup LAND O LAKES® Butter, melted

2 tablespoons sugar

Filling

1 cup sugar

4 (8 ounce) packages cream cheese, softened

4 eggs

1 (12 ounce) package (2 cups) vanilla milk chips, melted*

1 cup chocolate fudge topping, warmed

Sauce

2 (10 ounce) packages frozen raspberries in syrup, thawed

1 tablespoon cornstarch

Heat oven to 325°. In small bowl stir together all crust ingredients. Press crumb mixture evenly onto bottom of 9-inch springform pan. Bake 10 minutes; cool. In large mixer bowl combine 1 cup sugar and cream cheese. Beat at medium speed, scraping bowl often, until light and fluffy (3 to 4 minutes). Continue beating, adding eggs one at a time, until well mixed (1 to 2 minutes). Stir in melted vanilla milk chips. (Mixture may look lumpy.) Pour half of cream cheese mixture into prepared crust. Spoon 1/2 cup chocolate fudge topping over cream cheese mixture in crust; swirl with knife. Top with remaining cream cheese mixture. Spoon remaining chocolate fudge topping over cream cheese mixture; swirl with knife. Bake for 65 to 75 minutes or until just set 2 inches from edge of pan. Turn off oven; leave cheesecake in oven 2 hours.

Loosen sides of cheesecake from pan by running knife around inside of pan. Cool completely. Cover; refrigerate 8 hours or overnight. Meanwhile, press raspberries through strainer; discard seeds. (Strain raspberries again, if seeds still remain.) In 1-quart saucepan, with a wire whisk, stir together strained raspberries and cornstarch. Cook over medium heat, stirring constantly, until mixture comes to a full boil (4 to 8 minutes). Boil, stirring constantly, until slightly thickened (2 minutes). Remove from heat. Cool 5 minutes; stir. Cover; refrigerate until serving time. To serve, spoon raspberry sauce over each slice of cheesecake. Store refrigerated. **YIELD:** 12 servings.

*12 ounces white chocolate, chopped, can be substituted for 1 (12 ounce) package (2 cups) vanilla milk chips.

Nutrition Information (1 serving): Calories 700; Protein 12g; Carbohydrate 68g; Fat 44g; Cholesterol 165mg; Sodium 410mg.

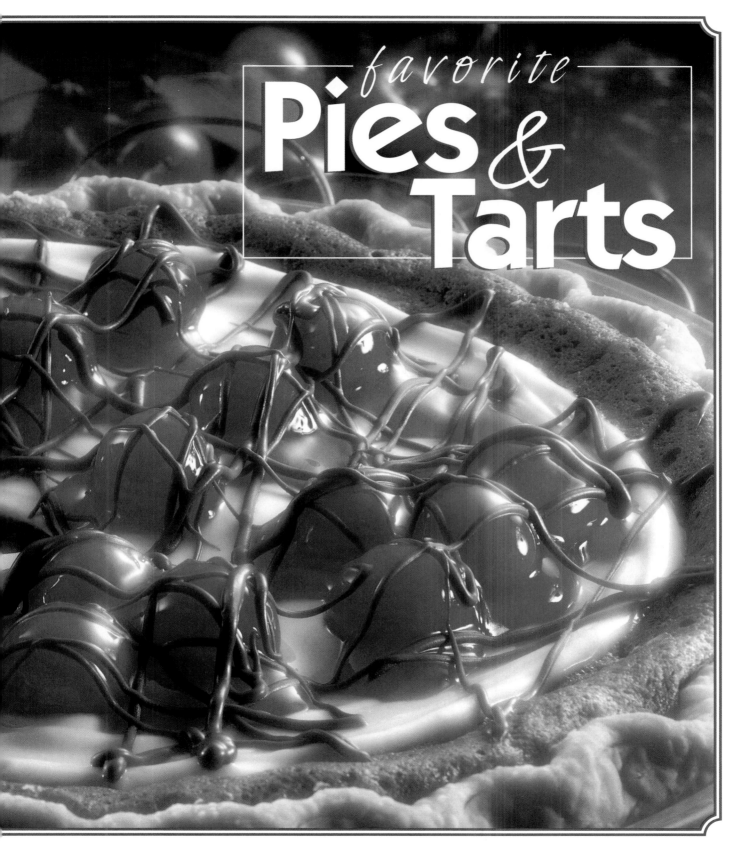

favorite
Pies & Tarts

Black Forest Pie

Black Forest Pie

*This fudge brownie pie is topped with
sour cream and cherries.*

Preparation time: 45 minutes • Bake time: 50 minutes • Chilling time: 2 hours

Single crust pie pastry*

Filling
3/4 cup
    LAND O LAKES® Butter
3/4 cup sugar
6 tablespoons unsweetened
    cocoa
2/3 cup ground blanched
    almonds
2 tablespoons all-purpose
    flour
3 eggs, separated
2 tablespoons water
1/4 cup sugar

Topping
1/3 cup LAND O LAKES®
    Light Sour Cream
2 tablespoons sugar
1/2 teaspoon vanilla
1 cup canned cherry pie
    filling

Glaze
1/2 cup semi-sweet real
    chocolate chips
1 1/2 teaspoons shortening

Heat oven to 350°. Place pastry in 9-inch pie pan. Crimp or flute crust; set aside. In 2-quart saucepan melt 3/4 cup butter over medium heat (3 to 5 minutes). Stir in 3/4 cup sugar and 6 tablespoons cocoa. Remove from heat; cool 5 minutes. Stir in almonds and flour. Stir in egg yolks, one at a time, until well mixed. Stir in 2 tablespoons water. In small mixer bowl beat egg whites at high speed, scraping bowl often, until foamy. Continue beating, gradually adding 1/4 cup sugar, until soft peaks form (30 to 60 seconds). Fold chocolate mixture into egg whites just until blended.

Pour into prepared pie shell. Bake for 35 to 45 minutes or until wooden pick inserted in center comes out clean. Cool 5 minutes. In medium bowl stir together all topping ingredients <u>except</u> cherry pie filling. Spread over warm pie; top with spoonfuls of cherry pie filling. Return pie to oven for 5 minutes. In 1-quart saucepan melt chocolate chips and shortening over low heat, stirring constantly, until melted (2 to 3 minutes). Drizzle over pie. Refrigerate at least 2 hours. **YIELD:** 10 servings.

*See crust recipe on page 137.

Nutrition Information (1 serving): Calories 460; Protein 6g; Carbohydrate 47g; Fat 30g; Cholesterol 120mg; Sodium 280mg.

Pie Pastry

A standard recipe for 9-inch pie pastry.

Preparation time: 30 minutes

Single Crust Pie Pastry

1 cup all-purpose flour
1/8 teaspoon salt
1/3 cup LAND O LAKES®
   Butter
3 to 4 tablespoons cold water

Double Crust Pie Pastry

2 cups all-purpose flour
1/4 teaspoon salt
2/3 cup LAND O LAKES®
   Butter
4 to 5 tablespoons cold water

In large bowl stir together flour and salt. Cut in butter until crumbly. With fork, mix in water until flour is just moistened. Shape into a ball. (For double crust divide pastry in half; shape each half into a ball.)

For single crust pie: On lightly floured surface roll out pastry ball into 12-inch circle. To transfer pastry to pie pan, fold pastry into quarters. Place in 9-inch pie pan with point in center. Gently unfold and ease into pie pan, pressing pastry gently with fingertips to fit snugly into pie pan. Crimp or flute edge. Fill and bake as directed in recipe.

For double crust pie: On lightly floured surface roll 1 pastry ball into 12-inch circle. To transfer pastry to pie pan, fold pastry into quarters. Place in 9-inch pie pan with point in center. Gently unfold and ease into pie pan, pressing pastry gently with fingertips to fit snugly into pie pan. Place desired filling in pastry-lined pie pan. Trim overhanging edge of pastry $1/2$ inch from rim of pie pan. Roll other pastry ball into 12-inch circle. Fold pastry into quarters. Place over filling; unfold. Trim overhanging edge of pastry 1 inch from rim of pie pan. Fold and roll top edge under lower edge, pressing on rim to seal; crimp or flute edge. Bake as directed in recipe.

For baked pie shell: Heat oven to 475°. Prepare and follow directions for single crust pie pastry. With fork, prick bottom and sides of pastry. Bake for 8 to 10 minutes or until lightly browned; cool.

Nutrition Facts ($1/8$ pastry) Single Crust: Calories 130; Protein 2g; Carbohydrate 12 g; Fat 8g; Cholesterol 20mg; Sodium 110mg

Nutrition Facts ($1/8$ pastry) Double Crust: Calories 250; Protein 3g; Carbohydrate 24g; Fat 16g; Cholesterol 40mg; Sodium 220mg

Choco-Peanut Butter Ice Cream Pie

Chocolate and peanut butter are mounded high
in this frozen ice cream pie.

Preparation time: 30 minutes • Baking time: 8 minutes • Cooling time: 15 minutes • Freezing time: 6 hours

Crust

1 1/2 cups graham cracker
  crumbs
3 tablespoons sugar
2 tablespoons chopped salted
  peanuts
1/4 cup
  LAND O LAKES® Butter,
  melted

Filling

2 cups chocolate ice cream,
  softened slightly
1 quart (4 cups) vanilla ice
  cream, slightly softened
1/3 cup peanut butter
2 tablespoons chopped salted
  peanuts

Chocolate syrup

Heat oven to 350°. In small bowl stir together all crust ingredients. Press on bottom and up sides of 9-inch or 10-inch pie pan. Bake for 6 to 8 minutes or until lightly browned. Cool completely. Spread softened chocolate ice cream over bottom of cooled pie crust. Freeze until firm (about 30 minutes). In large mixer bowl combine vanilla ice cream and peanut butter. Beat at low speed, scraping bowl often, until peanut butter is evenly distributed. Freeze until ice cream and peanut butter mixture holds soft mounds (30 to 45 minutes). Spoon ice cream and peanut butter mixture over chocolate ice cream layer. Spread to edges of crust, mounding slightly higher in center. Sprinkle with 2 tablespoons chopped peanuts. Freeze 4 to 5 hours or until firm. Let stand at room temperature 5 minutes before serving; drizzle with chocolate syrup. **YIELD:** 8 servings.

TIP: Do not use 8-inch pie pan.

Nutrition Information (1 serving): Calories 420; Protein 9g; Carbohydrate 43g; Fat 26g;
Cholesterol 61mg; Sodium 325mg.

Cherry Orchard Pie

*Grated orange peel spices this eye-catching
lattice-top cherry pie.*

Preparation time: 45 minutes • Baking time: 1 hour

Crust
2 cups all-purpose flour
1/4 teaspoon salt
2/3 cup
LAND O LAKES® Butter <u>or</u>
shortening
4 to 5 tablespoons cold water

Filling
1 cup sugar
1/3 cup all-purpose flour
1/8 teaspoon salt
2 (16 ounce) cans red tart
pitted cherries, drained
1 teaspoon grated orange peel

Milk
Sugar

Heat oven to 400°. In large bowl stir together 2 cups flour and 1/4 teaspoon salt. Cut in butter until crumbly. With fork mix in water until flour is moistened. Divide pastry in half; shape each half into a ball. On lightly floured surface roll 1 pastry ball into 12-inch circle. Place in 9-inch pie pan. Trim pastry to 1/2 inch from rim of pan; set aside. In large bowl combine sugar, 1/3 cup flour and 1/8 teaspoon salt. Add cherries and orange peel; toss lightly to coat. Spoon into prepared crust. With remaining half of pastry prepare lattice top. Roll pastry into 11-inch circle. With sharp knife or pastry wheel, cut circle into 10 (1/2-inch) strips. Place 5 strips, 1 inch apart, across filling in pie pan. Place remaining 5 strips, 1 inch apart, at right angles to the strips already in place. With kitchen shears, trim strips. Fold trimmed edge of bottom pastry over strips; build up an edge. Seal; crimp or flute edge. Brush strips with milk; sprinkle with sugar. Cover edge of crust with 2-inch strip of aluminum foil. Bake for 50 to 60 minutes or until crust is golden brown and filling bubbles in center. If desired, remove aluminum foil during last 5 minutes. If browning too quickly, shield lattice strips with aluminum foil. **YIELD:** 8 servings.

Nutrition Information (1 serving): Calories 420; Protein 5g; Carbohydrate 68g; Fat 16g; Cholesterol 41mg; Sodium 260mg.

Creamy Banana Pie with Lemon Zest

This heavenly banana cream pie is both light and luscious.

Preparation time: 1 hour • Baking time: 10 minutes • Cooling time: 30 minutes • Chilling time: 7 hours

Crust

1 cup all-purpose flour
1/8 teaspoon salt
1/3 cup
    LAND O LAKES® Butter
    or shortening
3 to 4 tablespoons cold water

Filling

3/4 cup sugar
1/4 cup cornstarch
1 (1/4 ounce) envelope
    unflavored gelatin
2 1/2 cups milk
4 egg yolks, slightly beaten
2 tablespoons
    LAND O LAKES® Butter
1 tablespoon vanilla
2 teaspoons grated lemon peel
2 tablespoons lemon juice
3 medium bananas, sliced
    1/4-inch
3/4 cup whipping cream

Topping

1/4 cup apple jelly
1 tablespoon lemon juice
1 medium banana, sliced
    1/4-inch

Heat oven to 475°. In large bowl stir together flour and salt. Cut in 1/3 cup butter until crumbly. With fork mix in water until flour is moistened. Shape into a ball. On lightly floured surface roll pastry ball into 12-inch circle. Place in 9-inch pie pan. Crimp or flute crust. With fork prick bottom and sides of pastry. Bake for 8 to 10 minutes or until lightly browned; cool completely. Meanwhile, in 2-quart saucepan combine sugar, cornstarch and gelatin. Gradually stir in milk and egg yolks. Cook over medium heat, stirring constantly, until mixture comes to a full boil (10 to 12 minutes). Stir in 2 tablespoons butter, vanilla and lemon peel until butter is melted; pour filling into large bowl. Cover; refrigerate until thickened (about 2 hours). Place 2 tablespoons lemon juice in small bowl; dip 3 sliced bananas into lemon juice. In chilled small mixer bowl beat chilled whipping cream, scraping bowl often, until stiff peaks form (1 to 2 minutes). By hand, fold whipped cream and bananas into pudding mixture. Pour into baked pie shell. Refrigerate at least 5 hours or until firm. Just before serving, in 1-quart saucepan stir together apple jelly and 1 tablespoon lemon juice. Cook over low heat, stirring occasionally, until apple jelly is melted (3 to 4 minutes). Arrange remaining banana slices 1 inch from outside edge of pie to form a circle. Spoon or drizzle apple jelly mixture over bananas. **YIELD:** 8 servings.

Nutrition Information (1 serving): Calories 470; Protein 8g; Carbohydrate 60g; Fat 23g; Cholesterol 174mg; Sodium 200mg.

Mixed Berry Meringue Pie

*Meringue forms the crust of this fresh
berry pie.*

Preparation time: 1 hour • Baking time: 1 hour 45 minutes • Cooling time: 1 hour • Chilling time: 2 hours

Meringue

2 egg whites
1/4 teaspoon cream of tartar
1/2 cup sugar

Filling

3/4 cup powdered sugar
1 cup LAND O LAKES®
  Light Sour Cream
4 ounces cream cheese
1 tablespoon orange juice
1 teaspoon grated orange
  peel

Topping

1 pint fresh strawberries,
  cleaned, hulled
1 cup fresh raspberries*
1/4 cup apple jelly, melted

Heat oven to 275°. In small mixer bowl combine egg whites and cream of tartar. Beat at high speed until foamy. Continue beating, gradually adding sugar and scraping bowl often, until glossy and stiff peaks form (3 to 4 minutes). Spoon into well greased (bottom only) 9-inch pie pan; using back of spoon, spread meringue over bottom and up sides. Bake for 1 hour. Turn off oven; leave meringue in oven with door closed for 45 minutes. Finish meringue cooling at room temperature. In small mixer bowl combine all filling ingredients. Beat at medium speed, scraping bowl often, until smooth and creamy (2 to 3 minutes). Spoon filling into meringue shell; using back of spoon spread over bottom and up sides. Refrigerate 2 hours or until firm. Just before serving, place strawberries, stem side down, on filling. Sprinkle raspberries over strawberries. Brush or drizzle melted apple jelly over berries. **YIELD:** 10 servings.

* 1 cup blueberries or combination of raspberries and blueberries can be
  substituted for 1 cup raspberries.

TIP: Meringue can be prepared day before serving.

*Nutrition Information (1 serving): Calories 180; Protein 4g; Carbohydrate 30g; Fat 6g;
Cholesterol 16mg; Sodium 73mg.*

Blue Ribbon Apple Pie

Pour whipping cream into this delectable apple pie; the cream thickens and settles around juicy apples.

Preparation time: 1 hour • Baking time: 1 hour • Cooling time: 30 minutes

Crust

2 cups all-purpose flour

1 teaspoon sugar

1/4 teaspoon salt

1/4 teaspoon cinnamon

1/4 teaspoon nutmeg

1/3 cup
LAND O LAKES® Butter

1/3 cup shortening

4 to 5 tablespoons cold water

Filling

1/2 cup sugar

1/4 cup firmly packed brown
sugar

1/4 cup all-purpose flour

1/2 teaspoon cinnamon

1/2 teaspoon nutmeg

6 cups (6 medium) peeled,
cored, sliced 1/4-inch tart
cooking apples

1 tablespoon
LAND O LAKES® Butter

1 teaspoon sugar

1/2 cup whipping cream

Heat oven to 400°. In large bowl stir together 2 cups flour, 1 teaspoon sugar, salt, 1/4 teaspoon cinnamon and 1/4 teaspoon nutmeg. Cut in 1/3 cup butter and shortening until crumbly. With fork mix in water until flour is moistened. Divide dough in half; shape into 2 balls and flatten. Wrap 1 ball in plastic food wrap; refrigerate. On lightly floured surface roll out other ball into 12-inch circle. Place in 9-inch pie pan. Trim pastry to 1/2-inch from rim of pan; set aside.

In large bowl combine all filling ingredients <u>except</u> apples, 1 tablespoon butter, 1 teaspoon sugar and whipping cream. Add apples; toss lightly to coat. Spoon into prepared crust. Roll remaining pastry ball into 12-inch circle; cut 8 large slits in top crust. Place over pie; crimp or flute crust. Brush with melted 1 tablespoon butter; sprinkle with 1 teaspoon sugar. Cover edge of crust with 2-inch strip of aluminum foil. Bake for 35 minutes; remove aluminum foil. Continue baking for 10 to 20 minutes or until crust is lightly browned and juice begins to bubble through slits in crust. Remove from oven; run knife through slits to open. Pour whipping cream evenly through all slits. Return to oven for 5 minutes to warm whipping cream. Cool pie 30 minutes; serve warm. **YIELD:** 8 servings.

TIP: If desired, omit whipping cream for a traditional apple pie.

Nutrition Information (1 serving): Calories 460; Protein 4g; Carbohydrate 60g; Fat 24g; Cholesterol 45mg; Sodium 170mg.

Chocolate-Laced Pecan Pie

*Two all-time favorites, pecan pie and chocolate,
come together in this extra-rich pie.*

Preparation time: 30 minutes • Baking time: 1 hour 45 minutes • Chilling time: 4 hours

Crust

1 cup all-purpose flour

1/8 teaspoon salt

1/3 cup
   LAND O LAKES® Butter or
   shortening

3 to 4 tablespoons cold water

Filling

2/3 cup sugar

1/3 cup
   LAND O LAKES® Butter,
   melted

1 cup light corn syrup

3 eggs

1/2 teaspoon salt

1 cup pecan halves

1/2 cup semi-sweet real
   chocolate chips

Pecan halves

Semi-sweet real chocolate
   chips, melted

Sweetened whipped cream

Heat oven to 375°. In large bowl stir together flour and 1/8 teaspoon salt. Cut in 1/3 cup butter until crumbly. With fork mix in water until flour is moistened. Shape into a ball. On lightly floured surface roll pastry ball into 12-inch circle. Place in 9-inch pie pan. Crimp or flute crust; set aside. In small mixer bowl combine sugar, 1/3 cup butter, corn syrup, eggs and 1/2 teaspoon salt. Beat at medium speed, scraping bowl often, until well mixed (1 to 2 minutes). By hand, stir in 1 cup pecans and 1/2 cup chocolate chips. Pour into prepared crust; if desired, turn pecan halves right side up. Cover pie loosely with aluminum foil. Bake for 30 minutes. Remove aluminum foil; continue baking for 10 to 15 minutes or until filling is set. If browning too quickly, re-cover with aluminum foil. Cool; refrigerate at least 4 hours or until ready to serve. If desired, dip additional pecan halves halfway in melted chocolate chips; refrigerate until set. Serve pie with sweetened whipped cream; garnish with dipped pecan halves.

YIELD: 8 servings.

TIP: If desired, omit semi-sweet chocolate chips for a traditional pecan pie.

*Nutrition Information (1 serving): Calories 640; Protein 6g; Carbohydrate 76g; Fat 37g;
Cholesterol 132mg; Sodium 380mg.*

Chocolate Silk Pie

This "smooth as silk" chocolate pie has a chocolate cookie crust
— a chocolate lover's delight.

Preparation time: 30 minutes • Chilling time: 3 hours

Crust

1 1/2 cups (about 18) finely
   crushed chocolate
   sandwich cookies
1/4 cup
   LAND O LAKES® Butter,
   melted

Filling

1 cup sugar
3/4 cup
   LAND O LAKES® Butter,
   slightly softened
3 (1 ounce) squares semi-sweet
   baking chocolate, melted,
   cooled
3/4 cup refrigerated
   pasteurized liquid eggs

Sweetened whipped cream
Chocolate curls

In medium bowl stir together crust ingredients. Press on bottom and up sides of 9-inch pie pan. Refrigerate 10 minutes. In small mixer bowl combine sugar and 3/4 cup butter. Beat at medium speed, scraping bowl often, until well mixed (1 to 2 minutes). Add chocolate; continue beating, scraping bowl often, until well mixed (1 to 2 minutes). Add eggs; continue beating, scraping bowl often, until light and fluffy (4 minutes). Spoon into prepared crust. Refrigerate at least 3 hours or until set. Garnish with sweetened whipped cream and chocolate curls. **YIELD:** 8 servings.

Nutrition Information (1 serving): Calories 490; Protein 4g; Carbohydrate 47g; Fat 34g; Cholesterol 90mg; Sodium 390mg.

Dixieland Peanut Pie

A taste of Southern tradition, peanut pie with whipped cream.

Preparation time: 45 minutes • Baking time: 40 minutes • Cooling time: 1 hour • Chilling time: 2 hours

Pastry
Single crust pie pastry*

Filling
1 cup firmly packed brown sugar

1 cup dark corn syrup

3 eggs

2 teaspoons vanilla

1 teaspoon lemon juice

1 cup coarsely chopped salted peanuts

1/2 cup whole salted peanuts

2 tablespoons LAND O LAKES® Butter

Sweetened whipped cream, if desired

Chopped peanuts, if desired

Heat oven to 375°. Line 9-inch pie pan with pastry. Crimp or flute edge; set aside.

In large mixer bowl combine brown sugar, corn syrup, eggs, vanilla and lemon juice. Beat at medium speed, scraping bowl often, until well mixed (1 to 2 minutes). By hand, stir in 1 cup chopped peanuts. Pour into prepared crust. Sprinkle top with 1/2 cup whole peanuts. Dot with 2 tablespoons butter. Bake for 40 to 45 minutes or until top of pie feels dry. If browning too quickly, cover with aluminum foil. Cool completely. Cover; refrigerate at least 2 hours. Garnish with sweetened whipped cream and chopped peanuts. **YIELD:** 8 servings.

*See crust recipe on page 137.

Nutrition Facts (1 serving): Calories 620; Protein 11g; Carbohydrate 78g; Fat 32g; Cholesterol 130mg; Sodium 440mg.

Easy Coconut Custard Pie

When there's little time to prepare dessert, bake this custard pie that forms its own crust during baking.

Preparation time: 10 minutes • Baking time: 40 minutes

2 cups milk

1 cup flaked coconut

³/4 cup sugar

¹/2 cup all-purpose flour

3 tablespoons
   LAND O LAKES®
   Butter, melted

4 eggs

1 teaspoon vanilla

Freshly grated whole
   nutmeg
Cut-up fresh fruit

Heat oven to 325°. In 5-cup blender container place milk; add all remaining ingredients <u>except</u> nutmeg and fruit. Cover; blend at medium speed until well mixed (1 to 2 minutes). Pour into greased and floured 9-inch pie pan; sprinkle with nutmeg. Bake for 40 to 45 minutes or until knife inserted in center comes out clean. Serve warm or chilled with fresh fruit. Store refrigerated. **YIELD:** 8 servings.

Nutrition Facts (1 serving): Calories 250; Protein 6g; Carbohydrate 32g; Fat 11g; Cholesterol 120mg; Sodium 130mg

Chewy Caramel-Brownie Pie

*This brownie pie is exceedingly rich, chewy, gooey and irresistible
when topped with a scoop of ice cream.*

Preparation time: 30 minutes • Baking time: 30 minutes • Standing time: 45 minutes

Brownie

1/2 cup
  LAND O LAKES® Butter
2 (1 ounce) squares
  unsweetened chocolate
1 cup sugar
3/4 cup all-purpose flour
2 eggs, slightly beaten
1/2 teaspoon salt
1/2 teaspoon baking powder
1 teaspoon vanilla

Caramel

8 ounces (30) caramels,
  unwrapped
3 tablespoons whipping
  cream
1/2 cup chopped pecans
1/4 cup semi-sweet real
  chocolate chips

Vanilla ice cream

Heat oven to 350°. In 2-quart saucepan combine butter and unsweetened chocolate. Cook over medium heat, stirring occasionally, until melted (4 to 6 minutes). Stir in all remaining brownie ingredients. Spread batter into greased 9-inch pie pan. Bake for 20 to 25 minutes or until brownie is firm to the touch. Meanwhile, in 1-quart saucepan heat caramels and whipping cream over medium low heat, stirring occasionally, until caramels are melted (5 to 6 minutes). Remove brownie from oven; spread melted caramel mixture over entire baked brownie. Sprinkle with pecans and chocolate chips. Continue baking for 3 to 5 minutes or until caramel mixture is bubbly. Let stand 30 to 45 minutes; cut into wedges. Serve warm with ice cream. **YIELD:** 8 servings.

Nutrition Information (1 serving): Calories 640; Protein 8g; Carbohydrate 79g; Fat 36g; Cholesterol 123mg; Sodium 410mg.

Pumpkin Squares

An easy way to serve pumpkin pie
to a crowd.

Preparation time: 30 minutes • Baking time: 1 hour

Crust
1 cup all-purpose flour
1/2 cup old-fashioned
   rolled oats
1/2 cup firmly packed
   brown sugar
1/2 cup
   LAND O LAKES® Butter,
   softened

Filling
3/4 cup sugar
1 (16 ounce) can pumpkin
1 (12 ounce) can evaporated
   milk
2 eggs
1 teaspoon cinnamon
1/2 teaspoon salt
1/2 teaspoon ginger
1/4 teaspoon cloves

Topping
1/2 cup firmly packed
   brown sugar
1/2 cup chopped pecans

Sweetened whipped cream

Heat oven to 350°. In small mixer bowl combine all crust ingredients. Beat at low speed, scraping bowl often, until crumbly (1 to 2 minutes). Press on bottom of 13x9-inch baking pan. Bake for 15 minutes. Meanwhile, in large mixer bowl combine all filling ingredients. Beat at medium speed, scraping bowl often, until smooth (1 to 2 minutes). Pour over crust; continue baking for 20 minutes. In small bowl stir together 1/2 cup brown sugar and pecans; sprinkle over filling. Continue baking for 15 to 25 minutes or until filling is firm to the touch or knife inserted in center comes out clean. Cool completely; cut into squares. Store refrigerated. **YIELD:** 12 servings.

Nutrition Information (1 serving): Calories 360; Protein 6g; Carbohydrate 49g; Fat 17g; Cholesterol 76mg; Sodium 220mg.

Strawberries 'N Cream Tart

Luscious ripe berries sit in
a delightful, fluffy cream.

Preparation time: 45 minutes • Baking time: 15 minutes • Cooling time: 30 minutes • Chilling time: 1 hour

Crust

1/2 cup
  LAND O LAKES® Butter,
  softened
1/3 cup sugar
1 1/4 cups all-purpose flour
2 tablespoons milk
1/2 teaspoon almond extract

Filling

1 (3 ounce) package cream
  cheese, softened
1/2 cup powdered sugar
1/2 teaspoon almond extract
1 cup whipping cream

Topping

1 pint fresh strawberries,
  sliced, <u>or</u> fresh raspberries
2 to 4 tablespoons strawberry
  <u>or</u> raspberry jelly, melted

Heat oven to 400°. In small mixer bowl beat butter and sugar at medium speed, scraping bowl often, until light and fluffy (1 to 2 minutes). Add flour, milk and 1/2 teaspoon almond extract. Reduce speed to low; continue beating, scraping bowl often, until mixture leaves sides of bowl and forms a ball. Press dough onto bottom and up sides of greased 10-inch tart pan or 12-inch pizza pan; prick with fork. Bake for 10 to 15 minutes or until light golden brown. Cool. In small mixer bowl combine cream cheese, powdered sugar and 1/2 teaspoon almond extract. Beat at medium speed, scraping bowl often, until light and fluffy (1 to 2 minutes). Continue beating, gradually adding whipping cream, until mixture is thick and fluffy (2 to 3 minutes). Spread over top of cooled crust. Refrigerate at least 1 hour. Just before serving, arrange fruit on filling. Brush or drizzle melted jelly over fruit. **YIELD:** 10 servings.

Nutrition Information (1 serving): Calories 320; Protein 3g; Carbohydrate 29g; Fat 22g; Cholesterol 68mg; Sodium 133mg.

Pear Custard Tart

A velvety custard bakes around slices of red, blushed pears in a flaky pastry tart.

Preparation time: 1 hour • Baking time: 51 minutes

Pastry

1 2/3 cups all-purpose flour
2 tablespoons sugar
3/4 cup
   LAND O LAKES® Butter
1 egg, slightly beaten
1 tablespoon milk

Filling

3/4 cup sugar
2 tablespoons cornstarch
2 cups milk
5 egg yolks, slightly beaten
2 tablespoons
   LAND O LAKES® Butter
2 teaspoons vanilla
1 tablespoon lemon juice
3 medium ripe red pears, sliced
   1/4-inch

Powdered sugar

Heat oven to 400°. In large bowl stir together flour and 2 tablespoons sugar. Cut in 3/4 cup butter until crumbly. With fork mix in egg and 1 tablespoon milk just until moistened. Shape into ball; on lightly floured surface roll into 14-inch circle. Place in 10-inch tart pan; press on bottom and up sides of pan. Cut away excess pastry. Prick with fork generously. Bake for 9 to 11 minutes or until lightly browned. Reduce oven to 375°. Meanwhile, in 2-quart saucepan combine 3/4 cup sugar and cornstarch. Gradually stir in 2 cups milk. Cook over medium heat, stirring constantly, until mixture is thickened and comes to a full boil (10 to 15 minutes). Boil, stirring constantly, 1 minute.

Place egg yolks in medium bowl; slowly whisk 2/3 of hot milk mixture into egg yolks. Return to same pan with remaining hot milk mixture. Continue cooking, stirring constantly, until mixture comes to a full boil (3 to 5 minutes). Boil, stirring constantly, 1 minute. Remove from heat; stir in 2 tablespoons butter and vanilla until butter is melted. Place lemon juice in small bowl; dip pear slices into lemon juice. Pour custard into baked pastry; arrange pear slices in custard. Bake for 30 to 40 minutes or until custard is set. Cool 1 hour before serving. Sprinkle with powdered sugar. **YIELD:** 8 servings.

Nutrition Information (1 serving): Calories 490; Protein 8g; Carbohydrate 56g; Fat 27g; Cholesterol 260mg; Sodium 250mg.

Macadamia Tart

Macadamia nuts have a unique flavor and texture. Because of their hard shells they are always sold already shelled.

Preparation time: 45 minutes • Chilling time: 1 hour 30 minutes • Baking time: 28 minutes • Cooling time: 1 hour

Pastry

1 cup all-purpose flour
1 tablespoon sugar
1/4 teaspoon salt
1/2 cup LAND O LAKES®
  Butter, chilled
2 to 3 tablespoons cold water

Filling

1 cup firmly packed brown
  sugar
1 tablespoon all-purpose
  flour
1 cup whipping cream
1/2 cup coarsely chopped
  macadamia nuts

Drizzle

2 tablespoons semi-sweet real
  chocolate chips
1/2 teaspoon shortening
Macadamia nuts, if desired

In medium bowl stir together 1 cup flour, sugar and salt. Cut in butter until crumbly. With fork, stir in water until flour is just moistened. Shape into a ball; wrap in plastic food wrap. Refrigerate 30 minutes.

Heat oven to 425°. On lightly floured surface roll pastry ball into 11-inch circle. Place in 10-inch tart pan with removable bottom. Press dough on bottom and sides of pan; crimp edge, trimming if needed. Bake for 8 to 10 minutes or until pastry is just beginning to brown.

In medium bowl stir together brown sugar and 1 tablespoon flour until well blended. Gradually stir in whipping cream. Pour into crust; sprinkle with $1/2$ cup macadamia nuts. Bake for 20 to 25 minutes or until filling is bubbly all over. Cool completely (1 to 2 hours).

In 1-quart saucepan melt chocolate chips and shortening over low heat, stirring constantly, until melted (1 to 2 minutes). Drizzle over tart. Garnish with macadamia nuts. Refrigerate at least 1 hour. Store refrigerated. **YIELD:** 10 servings.

Nutrition Facts (1 serving): Calories 360; Protein 3g; Carbohydrate 36g; Fat 24g; Cholesterol 55mg; Sodium 170mg.

Chocolate Peanut Butter Tart

The name alone describes this rich dessert that can be served as a tart or a bar.

Preparation time: 1 hour • Chilling time: 2 hours

Crust

1 1/2 cups graham cracker
   crumbs
1/3 cup unsalted peanuts,
   chopped
1/2 cup LAND O LAKES®
   Butter, melted

Fudge Layer

2 tablespoons
   LAND O LAKES® Butter
1 cup semi-sweet real chocolate
   chips
1 tablespoon water
1/4 cup powdered sugar

Filling

1/3 cup powdered sugar
1/2 cup creamy peanut butter
1/4 cup
   LAND O LAKES® Butter,
   softened
1 (3 ounce) package cream
   cheese, softened

Chocolate Drizzle

1 tablespoon
   LAND O LAKES® Butter
2 tablespoons semi-sweet real
   chocolate chips

In medium bowl stir together all crust ingredients. Press crust mixture evenly on bottom of 10-inch tart pan or pizza pan; refrigerate until firm (5 to 10 minutes). In 1-quart saucepan combine 2 tablespoons butter, 1 cup chocolate chips and water. Cook over medium heat, stirring occasionally, until melted (3 to 5 minutes). Remove from heat; stir in 1/4 cup powdered sugar until smooth. Spread fudge mixture over crust; set aside. In medium mixer bowl combine all filling ingredients. Beat at high speed, scraping bowl often, until light and fluffy (2 to 3 minutes). Spread peanut butter mixture over fudge layer. In 1-quart saucepan combine 1 tablespoon butter and 2 tablespoons chocolate chips. Cook over low heat, stirring constantly, until melted and smooth (2 to 3 minutes). Drizzle over filling. Cover; refrigerate at least 2 hours. **YIELD:** 16 servings.

VARIATION

Chocolate Peanut Butter Bars: Prepare recipe as directed above, using a 13x9-inch pan in place of 10-inch tart pan or pizza pan. **YIELD:** 32 bars.

Nutrition Information (1 serving): Calories 280; Protein 4g; Carbohydrate 19g; Fat 23g; Cholesterol 35mg; Sodium 220mg.

Blueberry Rhubarb Tart

Instead of strawberries, we've paired rhubarb with blueberries for a surprising taste.

Preparation time: 30 minutes • Baking time: 50 minutes • Cooling time: 1 hour

Crust
1	cup all-purpose flour
1	tablespoon sugar
1/4	teaspoon salt
1/4	cup LAND O LAKES® Butter
1/4	cup shortening
3	tablespoons water

Filling
1/2	cup sugar
3	tablespoons cornstarch
2	cups sliced 1/4-inch fresh <u>or</u> frozen rhubarb
2/3	cup apple juice
1	cup fresh <u>or</u> frozen blueberries

Sweetened whipped cream, if desired

Heat oven to 375°. In medium bowl stir together flour, 1 tablespoon sugar and salt. Cut in butter and shortening until crumbly. With fork, stir in water just until flour is moistened. Shape into a ball. On lightly floured surface roll ball into 10-inch circle. Place in 9-inch tart pan with removable bottom; press on bottom and up sides of pan. Bake for 10 minutes.

Meanwhile, in 2-quart saucepan combine 1/2 cup sugar and cornstarch. Gradually stir in rhubarb and apple juice. Cook over medium heat, stirring constantly, until thickened (5 to 7 minutes). Remove from heat; stir in blueberries. Pour into crust. Bake for 40 to 50 minutes or until center is bubbly. Cool completely. Using pastry bag, pipe whipped cream onto tart forming a lattice. **YIELD:** 8 servings.

Nutrition Facts (1 serving): Calories 280; Protein 2g; Carbohydrate 36g; Fat 15g; Cholesterol 25mg; Sodium 130mg

Stars & Stripes Tart

A rich fruit tart in celebration
of our patriotism.

Preparation time: 45 minutes • Baking time: 18 minutes • Cooling time: 30 minutes • Chilling time: 1 hour

Crust

1 cup
  LAND O LAKES® Butter,
  softened
1/2 cup sugar
2 1/2 cups all-purpose flour
1/3 cup milk

Filling

3 (3 ounce) packages cream
  cheese, softened
3/4 cup powdered sugar
1 teaspoon grated orange peel
1 tablespoon orange juice

Topping

1 pint strawberries, hulled,
  sliced <u>or</u> raspberries*
1 cup fresh blueberries*
1/4 cup apple jelly, melted

Heat oven to 400°. In large mixer bowl combine butter and sugar. Beat at medium speed, scraping bowl often, until light and fluffy (1 to 2 minutes). Add flour and milk; beat at low speed until well mixed. Press dough on bottom and 1/2 inch up sides of 13x9-inch baking pan. Prick bottom with fork. Bake for 14 to 18 minutes or until lightly browned. Cool. In small mixer bowl combine all filling ingredients; beat at medium speed, scraping bowl often, until light and fluffy (1 to 2 minutes). Spread over top of cooled crust. Refrigerate 1 hour or until firm. Just before serving, arrange fruit on filling in design of American flag, using strawberry slices for stripes and blueberries for stars. Brush fruit and filling with melted apple jelly. **YIELD:** 12 servings.

*4 cups of your favorite fruit (kiwi, mandarin orange segments, pineapple, etc.), arranged in any design, can be substituted for strawberries and blueberries.

Nutrition Information (1 serving): Calories 350; Protein 4g; Carbohydrate 44g; Fat 18g; Cholesterol 50mg; Sodium 184mg.

Raspberry Tart

Tender almond crust filled with luscious red raspberries.

Preparation time: 30 minutes • Chilling time: 1 hour • Baking time: 25 minutes

Crust

1¹/₂ cups all-purpose flour

¹/₂ cup sugar

¹/₂ cup **LAND O LAKES®** Butter, cut into 1-inch pieces

1 egg

1 teaspoon almond extract

¹/₂ cup finely chopped almonds

1 egg white, slightly beaten

Filling

3 cups fresh raspberries, washed, drained

2 tablespoons sugar

Ice cream *or* sweetened whipped cream, if desired

In large mixer bowl combine all crust ingredients <u>except</u> chopped almonds and egg white. Beat at medium speed, scraping bowl often, until mixture is crumbly (2 to 3 minutes). By hand, stir in almonds. Press on bottom and 1 inch up sides of 10-inch springform pan. Refrigerate 1 hour.

<u>Heat oven to 400°</u>. Brush crust with egg white. Bake for 15 minutes. Arrange raspberries in crust; continue baking for 10 to 15 minutes or until crust is golden brown. Sprinkle with 2 tablespoons sugar. Serve warm with ice cream or sweetened whipped cream.
YIELD: 8 servings.

Nutrition Facts (1 serving): Calories 460; Protein 8g; Carbohydrate 57g; Fat 24g; Cholesterol 90mg; Sodium 190mg

Crisp Phyllo Petals with Berries

The pastry of this luscious pie is made from phyllo dough, the filling from sweetened whipped cream and summer's berries.

Preparation time: 1 hour 15 minutes • Baking time: 12 minutes

Crust
6 sheets frozen phyllo dough, thawed
1/4 cup
  LAND O LAKES® Butter, melted
2 tablespoons powdered sugar

Filling
1 cup whipping cream
1/4 cup powdered sugar
2 tablespoons orange juice
1/2 teaspoon vanilla
4 cups (1 quart) fresh strawberries, hulled, sliced 1/4-inch
1 cup fresh raspberries
1 cup fresh blueberries
Powdered sugar

Heat oven to 400°. Lay one sheet of phyllo over 9-inch pie pan, gently gathering to form ruffled and uneven rim. Fit into pan, allowing ends to hang over. (Keep remaining phyllo sheets covered while assembling crust.) Brush phyllo with about 2 teaspoons melted butter; sprinkle with about 1 teaspoon powdered sugar. Fit second sheet of phyllo in pan at right angles to first. Brush with 2 teaspoons butter; sprinkle with 1 teaspoon powdered sugar. Repeat layering, buttering and sugaring with remaining phyllo sheets, butter and powdered sugar. Bake for 7 to 12 minutes or until golden brown. Let stand 5 minutes; remove from pan. Place on serving plate. Sprinkle powdered sugar over crust.

Just before serving, in chilled small mixer bowl beat chilled whipping cream at high speed, scraping bowl often, until soft peaks form (1 to 2 minutes). Continue beating, gradually adding 1/4 cup powdered sugar, until stiff peaks form (1 to 2 minutes). Fold in orange juice and vanilla. Fold in 2 cups strawberries, 1/2 cup raspberries and 1/2 cup blueberries. Spoon whipped cream mixture into center of crust. Arrange remaining berries on top of whipped cream mixture; sprinkle with powdered sugar. **YIELD:** 6 servings.

Nutrition Information (1 serving): Calories 310; Protein 3g; Carbohydrate 26g; Fat 23g; Cholesterol 75mg; Sodium 151mg.

Puff Pastry
Strawberry Lemon Tart

Strawberries complement a lemon curd filling encased in a delicate pastry shell.

Preparation time: 1 hour • Baking time: 15 minutes • Cooling time: 15 minutes • Chilling time: 2 hours 15 minutes

Pastry

1/2 (17 1/4-ounce) package
  (2 sheets) frozen puff
  pastry sheets, thawed
1 egg yolk, slightly beaten

Filling

2/3 cup sugar
1/2 cup LAND O LAKES®
  Butter
1/4 cup lemon juice
3 egg yolks
1 tablespoon cornstarch
1 tablespoon grated lemon
  peel

1 pint strawberries, washed,
  hulled, cut in half
Sweetened whipped cream

On lightly floured surface roll out pastry into 14x9-inch rectangle. Cut out 8-inch circle from dough. Using 2-inch round cookie cutter cut 6 circles from remaining dough. Cut 2-inch circles in half. Sprinkle cookie sheet with cold water; place 8-inch circle on cookie sheet. Brush pastry with beaten egg yolk; prick dough with fork. Place half-circles around outside edge of pastry. Brush with remaining egg yolk. Refrigerate 15 minutes.

Heat oven to 425°. Bake for 15 to 17 minutes or until golden brown. Cool completely.

In 2-quart saucepan combine all filling ingredients. Cook over medium heat, stirring constantly, until mixture comes to a full boil (5 to 6 minutes). Boil 1 minute. Cover surface with plastic food wrap; cool to room temperature. Pour filling into pastry; refrigerate until firm (2 to 3 hours).

To serve, arrange strawberries on top of filling and garnish with sweetened whipped cream. **YIELD:** 8 servings.

Nutrition Facts (1 serving): Calories 380; Protein 4g; Carbohydrate 34g; Fat 27g; Cholesterol 160mg; Sodium 240mg

*I*ndividual *P*lum *T*arts

Use ripe red plums in this recipe for best flavor.

Preparation time: 35 minutes • Baking time: 25 minutes • Cooling time: 30 minutes

Tart Shells

    2   tablespoons sugar
 1/2   teaspoon cinnamon
    1   (17 1/4-ounce) package
        (2 sheets) frozen puff
        pastry sheets, thawed
 1/4   cup LAND O LAKES®
        Butter, melted

Plum Filling

 1/4   cup sugar
 1/4   cup LAND O LAKES®
        Butter
    6   medium plums, sliced,
        pitted
 1/2   teaspoon cinnamon

Cream Filling

 1/2   cup powdered sugar
    1   (8-ounce) package cream
        cheese, softened
    2   tablespoons milk
    1   teaspoon vanilla

Heat oven to 350°. In small bowl combine 2 tablespoons sugar and 1/2 teaspoon cinnamon; set aside.

On lightly floured surface cut each sheet of puff pastry into 4 (5-inch) squares. Fold each square in half diagonally forming a triangle. Starting at folded side cut 1/2-inch border strip on both sides of triangle leaving 3/4 inch uncut at point so strips remain attached. Unfold triangle. Lift both cut border strips and pull one under the other, pulling to match corners on base. Brush with butter; sprinkle with sugar mixture. Prick all over center of each square with fork. Place on 2 cookie sheets. Bake for 25 to 30 minutes or until golden brown. Cool completely.

Meanwhile, in 10-inch skillet place all plum filling ingredients. Cook over medium heat, stirring occasionally, until plums are tender and juice is slightly thickened (5 to 8 minutes). Cool to room temperature (30 to 45 minutes).

In small mixer bowl combine all cream filling ingredients. Beat at medium speed, scraping bowl often, until smooth (2 to 3 minutes). Cover; refrigerate until serving time.

To serve, place each baked tart shell on individual dessert plate. Spread bottom of each tart shell with about 2 tablespoons cream filling. Divide plums among tarts; drizzle with plum filling liquid. **YIELD:** 8 servings.

Nutrition Facts (1 serving): Calories 590; Protein 7g; Carbohydrate 52g; Fat 41g; Cholesterol 80mg; Sodium 440mg

irresistible
Desserts

Individual Fruit-Filled Meringues and Salted Peanut Ice Cream Squares

Individual Fruit-Filled Meringues

These heart-shaped meringues showcase a cloud of whipped cream and a colorful arrangement of fresh fruit.

Preparation time: 30 minutes • Baking time: 1 hour • Cooling time: 1 hour 30 minutes

Meringues
4 egg whites
2 teaspoons cornstarch
1/4 teaspoon cream of tartar
1 teaspoon lemon juice
1 cup sugar
1/3 cup powdered sugar

Whipped Cream
1 cup whipping cream
1/4 cup sugar
1 teaspoon vanilla

1 cup sliced fresh strawberries
1 cup 1-inch pieces fresh
   pineapple
1 kiwi, cut into 6 slices

Heat oven to 275°. In large mixer bowl beat egg whites, cornstarch, cream of tartar and lemon juice at high speed, scraping bowl often, until soft peaks form (1 to 2 minutes). Continue beating, gradually adding 1 cup sugar and powdered sugar, until glossy and stiff peaks form (6 to 8 minutes). On brown paper or parchment paper-lined cookie sheet, shape or pipe 6 (about 4-inch) individual heart-shaped or round meringues, building up sides. Bake for 1 hour. Turn off oven; leave meringues in oven with door closed for 1 hour. Finish cooling meringues at room temperature. In chilled small mixer bowl beat chilled whipping cream at high speed, scraping bowl often, until soft peaks form. Continue beating, gradually adding 1/4 cup sugar, until stiff peaks form (1 to 2 minutes). By hand, fold in vanilla. Fill meringue shells with whipped cream; top with strawberries, pineapple and kiwi. **YIELD:** 6 servings.

Nutrition Information (1 serving): Calories 370; Protein 4g; Carbohydrate 57g; Fat 15g; Cholesterol 54mg; Sodium 55mg.

Salted Peanut Ice Cream Squares

*A sure hit, the flavors in this frozen dessert are similar
to a popular candy bar.*

Preparation time: 30 minutes • Freezing time: 4 hours

1/2 cup light corn syrup

1/2 cup chunky-style
  peanut butter

3 cups crisp rice cereal

1/2 gallon vanilla ice cream,
  slightly softened*

1 cup chopped salted peanuts

Caramel ice cream topping

In large bowl stir together corn syrup and peanut butter. Stir in cereal. Press on bottom of buttered 13x9-inch pan; freeze until firm (about 10 minutes). Spread ice cream on top of crust; sprinkle with chopped peanuts. Pat into ice cream. Cover; freeze until firm (2 to 4 hours). To serve, in 1-quart saucepan heat caramel topping. Cut ice cream into squares; serve caramel topping over ice cream. **YIELD:** 12 servings.

* 1/2 gallon chocolate chip, praline pecan or your favorite flavor ice cream can be substituted for 1/2 gallon vanilla ice cream.

*Nutrition Information (1 serving): Calories 410; Protein 10g; Carbohydrate 48g; Fat 21g;
Cholesterol 40mg; Sodium 294mg.*

Tea Biscuits with Blushing Raspberries

*Light, tender biscuits are topped with
ruby red raspberries.*

Preparation time: 25 minutes • Baking time: 14 minutes

Biscuits

2 cups all-purpose flour
1/2 cup sugar
1 tablespoon baking powder
1/2 teaspoon salt
2/3 cup
   LAND O LAKES® Butter
1/2 cup whipping cream
2 tablespoons orange juice

Whipped Cream

1 cup whipping cream
2 tablespoons sugar
1 teaspoon vanilla

Raspberry Sauce

1 pint fresh raspberries*
1/3 cup powdered sugar
1/4 cup orange juice

1 pint fresh raspberries

Heat oven to 400°. In large bowl combine flour, 1/2 cup sugar, baking powder and salt. Cut in butter until crumbly. Stir in 1/2 cup whipping cream and 2 tablespoons orange juice just until moistened. Turn dough onto lightly floured surface; knead until smooth (1 minute). Roll out dough to 1/2-inch thickness. With 2-inch scalloped round or heart-shaped cutter, cut out 8 biscuits. Place 1-inch apart on cookie sheet. Bake for 10 to 14 minutes or until lightly browned.

Meanwhile, in chilled small mixer bowl beat chilled 1 cup whipping cream at high speed, scraping bowl often, until soft peaks form. Continue beating, gradually adding 2 tablespoons sugar, until stiff peaks form (1 to 2 minutes). By hand, fold in vanilla. In 5-cup blender container place 1 pint raspberries, powdered sugar and 1/4 cup orange juice. Blend on High speed until pureed (1 to 2 minutes). If desired, strain sauce to remove seeds. Place biscuits in individual dessert dishes. Serve with raspberry sauce, whipped cream and fresh raspberries. **YIELD:** 8 servings.

*1 (10 ounce) package frozen raspberries can be substituted for 1 pint fresh raspberries.

Nutrition Information (1 serving): Calories 520; Protein 5g; Carbohydrate 55g; Fat 33g; Cholesterol 103mg; Sodium 420mg.

Granny's Peaches & Cream Cobbler

*This irresistible cobbler brings memories of visits to
Grandma's house.*

Preparation time: 30 minutes • Baking time: 45 minutes

Filling

1 cup sugar

2 eggs, slightly beaten

2 tablespoons all-purpose flour

1/2 teaspoon nutmeg

4 cups (4 to 6 medium) peeled,
   sliced fresh peaches*

Cobbler

1 1/2 cups all-purpose flour

2 tablespoons sugar

1 teaspoon baking powder

1/2 teaspoon salt

1/3 cup
   LAND O LAKES® Butter,
   softened

1 egg, slightly beaten

3 tablespoons milk

3 tablespoons sugar

Whipping cream

Heat oven to 400°. In large bowl stir together all filling ingredients <u>except</u> peaches. Stir in peaches. Pour into 13x9-inch baking pan. In medium bowl stir together all cobbler ingredients <u>except</u> butter, egg and milk. Cut in butter until crumbly. Stir in egg and milk just until moistened. Crumble mixture over peaches; sprinkle with 3 tablespoons sugar. Bake for 40 to 45 minutes or until golden brown and bubbly around edges. Serve with whipping cream. **YIELD:** 8 servings.

*2 (16 ounce) packages sliced frozen peaches can be substituted for 4 cups sliced fresh peaches.

Nutrition Information (1 serving): Calories 410; Protein 6g; Carbohydrate 63g; Fat 16g; Cholesterol 122mg; Sodium 280mg.

Apple Dumplings & Brandy Sauce

*A tender butter crust, baked to a golden brown, surrounds
these pecan-filled apple dumplings smothered in a rich sauce.*

Preparation time: 1 hour • Baking time: 50 minutes

Dumplings

2 cups all-purpose flour
1/4 teaspoon salt
1/2 cup
  LAND O LAKES® Butter,
  cut into pieces
2/3 cup LAND O LAKES®
  Light Sour Cream
6 medium tart cooking
  apples, cored, peeled
1/3 cup sugar
1/3 cup chopped pecans
2 tablespoons
  LAND O LAKES® Butter,
  softened
Milk

Sauce

1/2 cup firmly packed brown
  sugar
2 tablespoons
  LAND O LAKES® Butter
1/2 cup whipping cream
1 tablespoon brandy*

Heat oven to 400°. In medium bowl stir together flour and salt. Cut in 1/2 cup butter until mixture forms coarse crumbs. With fork, stir in Light Sour Cream until mixture leaves sides of bowl and forms a ball. On lightly floured surface roll dough into 19x12-inch rectangle. Cut 1-inch strip off 19-inch end; reserve. Cut remaining dough into 6 (6-inch) squares. Place apple in center of each square. In small bowl stir together sugar, pecans and 2 tablespoons butter. Stuff <u>1 1/2 tablespoons</u> of mixture into cored center of each apple. Fold dough up around apple; seal seams well. Place, seam side down, on greased 15x10x1-inch jelly roll pan. Brush dough with milk; prick dough with fork.

Cut leaf designs out of reserved 1-inch strip of dough. Brush with milk; place on wrapped apples. Bake for 35 to 50 minutes or until apples are fork-tender. If crust browns too quickly, cover with aluminum foil. In 1-quart saucepan combine all sauce ingredients. Cook over medium heat, stirring occasionally, until mixture comes to a full boil (3 to 4 minutes). Serve sauce over warm dumplings. **YIELD:** 6 servings.

*1 teaspoon brandy extract can be substituted for 1 tablespoon brandy.

Nutrition Information (1 serving): Calories 690; Protein 7g; Carbohydrate 87g; Fat 37g; Cholesterol 96mg; Sodium 360mg.

Glazed Fruit Cups

Pretty pastry cups are filled with
orange-flavored fruits.

Preparation time: 1 hour • Baking time: 18 minutes

Cups

2 cups all-purpose flour

1/4 teaspoon salt

2/3 cup
  LAND O LAKES® Butter

4 to 5 tablespoons cold water

1 teaspoon grated orange peel

Filling

1/4 cup sugar

2 teaspoons cornstarch

1/2 cup orange juice

2 tablespoons
  LAND O LAKES® Butter

1 1/2 cups cut-up fresh fruit
  (bananas, grapes,
  raspberries, strawberries,
  peaches, etc.)

Red raspberry preserves,
  melted

Heat oven to 400°. In large bowl stir together flour and salt. Cut in 2/3 cup butter until crumbly; with fork, stir in water and orange peel until dough leaves sides of bowl and forms a ball. Roll out dough on well-floured surface to 1/8-inch thickness. Cut into 10 (4 1/2-inch) circles. Fit pastry into muffin cups; flute edges. With fork, prick bottom and sides of each cup. Bake for 14 to 18 minutes or until lightly browned. Cool; remove from pan. In 2-quart saucepan stir together sugar and cornstarch. Add orange juice. Cook over medium heat, stirring occasionally, until mixture comes to a full boil (5 to 8 minutes). Boil 2 minutes. Remove from heat. Stir in 2 tablespoons butter until melted. Gently stir in fruit. Spoon fruit mixture into each cup. If desired, top each cup with about 1 teaspoon melted raspberry preserves. **YIELD:** 10 servings.

TIP: Pastry cups can be made one day ahead.

Nutrition Information (1 serving): Calories 280; Protein 3g; Carbohydrate 34g; Fat 15g; Cholesterol 39mg; Sodium 203mg.

Raspberry Cream Cheese Turnovers

*Serve this raspberry cream pastry for
brunch or dessert.*

Preparation time: 1 hour • Chilling time: 30 minutes • Baking time: 25 minutes

Pastry

2 1/2 cups all-purpose flour
2/3 cup
   LAND O LAKES® Butter
1/2 cup LAND O LAKES®
   Light Sour Cream
4 to 6 tablespoons water

Filling

1 (3 ounce) package cream
   cheese, softened
1 egg yolk
2 tablespoons sugar
1 teaspoon all-purpose flour
1/2 teaspoon almond extract
1/4 cup raspberry preserves

Topping

2 tablespoons
   LAND O LAKES® Butter,
   melted
2 tablespoons sugar

Glaze

1/2 cup powdered sugar
1 tablespoon milk
1/4 teaspoon almond extract

In large bowl cut 2/3 cup butter into 2 1/2 cups flour until crumbly; stir in Light Sour Cream. With fork mix in water, 1 tablespoon at a time, until flour mixture is moistened. Divide dough in half; shape into 2 balls and flatten. Cover; refrigerate 30 minutes. <u>Heat oven to 400°</u>.

In medium bowl stir together all filling ingredients <u>except</u> raspberry preserves until smooth. On lightly floured surface roll out half of dough into 12x8-inch rectangle. Cut into six 4-inch squares. In center of each square place <u>2 teaspoons</u> filling and <u>1 teaspoon</u> raspberry preserves. Fold one corner of dough over filling to form a triangle. Seal edges with fork. Place on lightly greased cookie sheets. Repeat with remaining dough and filling. Brush tops of turnovers with 2 tablespoons melted butter; sprinkle with 2 tablespoons sugar. Bake for 20 to 25 minutes or until light golden brown. In small bowl stir together all glaze ingredients until smooth; drizzle over warm turnovers. Serve warm.
YIELD: 12 servings.

Nutrition Information (1 serving): Calories 290; Protein 4g; Carbohydrate 34g; Fat 16g; Cholesterol 61mg; Sodium 150mg.

Poached Pears with Raspberry & Chocolate Sauce

Ripe pears poached in wine are complemented
with two sauces.

Preparation time: 30 minutes • Cooking time: 43 minutes • Cooling time: 20 minutes

Pears

1/3 cup sugar

1 1/2 cups sauterne wine
or white grape juice

1 1/2 cups water

4 medium ripe pears, peeled,
leave stems on

Sauce

1 (10 ounce) package frozen
raspberries in syrup, thawed

2 teaspoons cornstarch

1 cup chocolate flavored syrup

4 teaspoons chopped
slivered almonds

In Dutch oven combine all pear ingredients. Cook over medium-high heat until mixture comes to a full boil (4 to 5 minutes). Reduce heat to medium; cover. Continue cooking, basting often, until pears are fork tender (20 to 30 minutes). Cool 15 minutes; drain. Cover pears; refrigerate until serving time or serve at room temperature. Meanwhile, press raspberries through strainer; discard seeds. (Strain raspberries again if seeds still remain.) In 1-quart saucepan, with wire whisk, stir together strained raspberries and cornstarch. Cook over medium heat, stirring constantly, until mixture comes to a full boil (3 to 6 minutes). Boil, stirring constantly, until slightly thickened (2 minutes). Remove from heat. Cool 5 minutes; stir. Cover; refrigerate until serving time. To serve, spoon 2 to 3 tablespoons chocolate syrup onto each of 4 individual serving plates. Cut thin slice off bottom of each pear. Stand pears upright in chocolate sauce. Spoon 1 to 2 tablespoons raspberry sauce over top of each pear, allowing sauce to drizzle down sides of pear; sprinkle with 1 teaspoon almonds. **YIELD:** 4 servings.

Nutrition Information (1 serving): Calories 390; Protein 3g; Carbohydrate 94g; Fat 3g;
Cholesterol 0mg; Sodium 75mg.

Apricot-Laced Cream Puffs

*An apricot cream cheese filling provides an interesting twist
to classic cream puffs.*

Preparation time: 1 hour • Baking time: 40 minutes • Cooling time: 30 minutes

Cream Puffs

1 cup water

1/2 cup
   LAND O LAKES® Butter

1 cup all-purpose flour

4 eggs

Apricot Cream

1/2 cup whipping cream

1/4 cup powdered sugar

1 (8 ounce) package
   cream cheese, softened

1/2 teaspoon ginger

2 tablespoons apricot
   preserves

1/2 cup apricot preserves,
   melted

Powdered sugar

Heat oven to 400°. In 2-quart saucepan bring water and butter to a full boil. Stir in flour. Cook over low heat, stirring vigorously, until mixture forms a ball. Add eggs, one at a time, beating until smooth. Drop about 1/3 cup dough 3 inches apart onto cookie sheet. Bake for 35 to 40 minutes or until puffed and golden brown. Cool completely. In chilled small mixer bowl beat chilled whipping cream at high speed, scraping bowl often, until soft peaks form. Continue beating, gradually adding 1/4 cup powdered sugar, until stiff peaks form (1 to 2 minutes). Add remaining apricot cream ingredients except 1/2 cup apricot preserves and powdered sugar. Continue beating, scraping bowl often, until smooth (2 to 3 minutes). Cut off cream puff tops; pull out any filaments of soft dough. Fill puffs with apricot cream; replace tops. Drizzle with melted apricot preserves; sprinkle with powdered sugar. **YIELD:** 8 servings.

Nutrition Information (1 serving): Calories 430; Protein 7g; Carbohydrate 34g; Fat 30g; Cholesterol 189mg; Sodium 240mg.

Blueberry Pan Pastries

Easier than old-fashioned dumplings. Try your family's favorite flavor pie filling in this homey dessert.

Preparation time: 30 minutes • Baking time: 45 minutes

Pastry
- 2 cups all-purpose flour
- 2 teaspoons baking powder
- $1/2$ teaspoon salt
- $2/3$ cup shortening
- $1/2$ cup milk

Filling
- 1 (21-ounce) can blueberry pie filling

Syrup
- $1/2$ cup sugar
- 1 cup water
- 3 tablespoons LAND O LAKES® Butter
- 1 tablespoon lemon juice
- 2 teaspoons grated lemon peel

Topping
- Vanilla ice cream, if desired

Heat oven to 375°. In medium bowl stir together flour, baking powder and salt. Cut in shortening until mixture resembles coarse crumbs. With fork, mix in milk until dough forms a ball. Divide in half. On lightly floured surface roll half of dough to 12-inch square. Cut into 4 (6-inch) squares.

Place about $1/4$ cup pie filling in center of each square. Fold dough up around filling; pinch edges to seal well. Place in 13x9-inch baking pan. Repeat with remaining dough. Bake for 30 to 35 minutes or until lightly browned.

Meanwhile, in 1-quart saucepan combine all syrup ingredients except ice cream. Cook over medium high heat until mixture comes to a full boil (3 to 5 minutes). Pour hot syrup over pastries. Continue baking until pastries are deep golden brown and syrup is slightly thickened (15 to 20 minutes). Serve warm with ice cream. **YIELD:** 8 servings.

TIP: 1 (21-ounce) can of your favorite flavor pie filling can be substituted for 1 (21-ounce) can blueberry pie filling.

Nutrition Facts (1 serving without ice cream): Calories 440; Protein 4g; Carbohydrate 58g; Fat 22g; Cholesterol 10mg; Sodium 270mg

Chocolate Chip Biscuits with Strawberries 'N Bananas

A tender biscuit is split and filled with whipped cream and sliced bananas.

Preparation time: 45 minutes • Baking time: 10 minutes

Biscuits

- 2 cups all-purpose flour
- $1/2$ cup sugar
- 1 tablespoon baking powder
- $1/2$ teaspoon salt
- $1/2$ cup LAND O LAKES® Butter
- $1/4$ cup shortening
- $2/3$ cup whipping cream
- $1/2$ cup coarsely chopped semi-sweet chocolate chips*

Whipped Cream

- $1^1/3$ cups whipping cream
- 3 tablespoons powdered sugar
- 1 teaspoon vanilla

- 1 pint strawberries, hulled, sliced
- 2 tablespoons sugar
- 2 bananas

Heat oven to 400°. In large bowl combine flour, $1/2$ cup sugar, baking powder and salt. Cut in butter and shortening until crumbly. With fork, stir in $2/3$ cup whipping cream just until moistened. Stir in chopped chocolate chips. Turn dough onto lightly floured surface; knead until smooth (1 minute). Roll out dough to $3/4$-inch thickness. With $2^1/2$-inch scalloped round cutter cut out 8 biscuits. Place 1 inch apart on cookie sheet. Bake for 10 to 14 minutes or until lightly browned.

Meanwhile, in chilled small mixer bowl beat $1^1/3$ cups chilled whipping cream at high speed, scraping bowl often, until soft peaks form. Continue beating, gradually adding powdered sugar and vanilla, until stiff peaks form (1 to 2 minutes).

In medium bowl place sliced strawberries; toss with 2 tablespoons sugar. To serve, split biscuits; place on individual dessert plates. Spoon whipped cream on bottom half of biscuits; place banana slices on whipped cream. Top with remaining half of biscuits; spoon strawberries over biscuits. **YIELD:** 8 servings.

*3 (1-ounce) squares coarsely chopped semi-sweet chocolate or $1/2$ cup miniature chocolate chips can be substituted for $1/2$ cup coarsely chopped chocolate chips.

TIP: To make chocolate whipped cream, $1/2$ cup semi-sweet real chocolate chips, melted, cooled, can be added to whipping cream after stiff peaks are formed. Continue beating until well mixed.

Nutrition Facts (1 serving): Calories 640; Protein 6g; Carbohydrate 60g; Fat 44g; Cholesterol 110mg; Sodium 390mg

Fudge Fantasy with Hazelnut Sauce

Chocolate is used in this rich, creamy dessert to contrast with the sweet, nutty sauce.

Preparation time: 30 minutes • Cooking time: 4 minutes • Baking time: 22 minutes • Cooling time: 1 hour

Fudge

2 1/2   cups semi-sweet real chocolate chips

1/2   cup LAND O LAKES® Butter

2   tablespoons all-purpose flour

2   tablespoons sugar

2   tablespoons hazelnut-flavored liqueur, if desired

4   eggs, slightly beaten

Sauce

1/2   cup firmly packed brown sugar

1/2   cup light corn syrup

1/4   cup LAND O LAKES® Butter

1/2   cup chopped toasted hazelnuts

1   tablespoon hazelnut-flavored liqueur, if desired

1   teaspoon vanilla

Whipped cream, if desired

Heat oven to 400°. Grease bottom and sides of 8-inch springform pan; dust with powdered sugar. In 2-quart saucepan cook chocolate chips and 1/2 cup butter over low heat, stirring constantly, until chocolate chips are melted (4 to 5 minutes). Stir in flour, sugar and 2 tablespoons liqueur. Stir in eggs until well mixed. Pour into prepared pan. Bake for 22 to 28 minutes or until fudge begins to pull away from sides of pan. Cool completely.

Meanwhile, in 1-quart saucepan combine brown sugar, corn syrup and 1/4 cup butter. Cook over medium heat, stirring occasionally, until mixture comes to a full boil (4 to 5 minutes). Boil 1 minute. Remove from heat; stir in hazelnuts, 1 tablespoon liqueur and vanilla. Cut fudge into wedges; top with sauce and whipped cream.

YIELD: 10 servings (1 1/2 cups sauce).

Nutrition Facts (1 serving): Calories 530; Protein 6g; Carbohydrate 52g; Fat 37g; Cholesterol 130mg; Sodium 180mg

Old-Fashioned Bread Pudding with Vanilla Sauce

Warm your heart with memories while enjoying this old-fashioned bread pudding.

Preparation time: 10 minutes • Baking time: 40 minutes • Cooking time: 5 minutes

Pudding

- 4 cups (8 slices) cubed white bread
- 1/2 cup raisins
- 2 cups milk
- 1/4 cup LAND O LAKES® Butter
- 1/2 cup sugar
- 2 eggs, slightly beaten
- 1/2 teaspoon ground nutmeg
- 1 teaspoon vanilla

Sauce

- 1/2 cup sugar
- 1/2 cup firmly packed brown sugar
- 1/2 cup LAND O LAKES® Butter
- 1/2 cup whipping cream
- 1 teaspoon vanilla

Heat oven to 350°. In large bowl combine bread and raisins. In 1-quart saucepan combine milk and 1/4 cup butter. Cook over medium heat until butter is melted (4 to 7 minutes). Pour milk mixture over bread; let stand 10 minutes. Stir in all remaining pudding ingredients. Pour into greased 1 1/2-quart casserole. Bake for 40 to 50 minutes or until set in center.

In 1-quart saucepan combine all sauce ingredients <u>except</u> vanilla. Cook over medium heat, stirring occasionally, until mixture thickens and comes to a full boil (5 to 8 minutes). Stir in vanilla. To serve, spoon warm pudding into individual dessert dishes; spoon sauce over. Store refrigerated. **YIELD:** 8 servings (1 1/2 cups sauce).

Nutrition Facts (1 serving): Calories 470; Protein 6g; Carbohydrate 56g; Fat 26g; Cholesterol 125mg; Sodium 310mg

Chocolate Hazelnut Truffle Dessert

*Serve a thin slice of this rich, dense chocolate dessert
with a creamy custard sauce.*

Preparation time: 1 hour • Freezing time: 8 hours • Cooking time: 11 minutes

Truffle Dessert
1 cup whipping cream
1/4 cup
   LAND O LAKES® Butter
2 (8 ounce) bars semi-sweet
   chocolate
4 egg yolks
3/4 cup powdered sugar
3 tablespoons rum <u>or</u>
   orange juice
1 cup coarsely chopped
   hazelnuts <u>or</u> filberts, toasted

Custard
1 cup whipping cream
1/4 cup sugar
1 teaspoon cornstarch
3 egg yolks
1 teaspoon vanilla

Garnish
Finely chopped hazelnuts

In 2-quart saucepan combine 1 cup whipping cream, butter and chocolate. Cook over medium heat, stirring occasionally, until chocolate is melted (5 to 7 minutes). With wire whisk stir in 4 egg yolks, one at a time. Continue cooking, stirring constantly, until mixture reaches 160° and thickens slightly (3 to 4 minutes). Remove from heat; whisk in powdered sugar and rum. Stir in hazelnuts. Line 8x4-inch loaf pan with aluminum foil, leaving 1-inch of aluminum foil over each edge. Pour chocolate mixture into prepared pan. Freeze 8 hours or overnight. In 2-quart saucepan cook 1 cup whipping cream over medium heat until mixture just comes to a boil (4 to 6 minutes). Remove from heat.

Meanwhile, in medium bowl combine sugar and cornstarch. Whisk in 3 egg yolks until mixture is light and creamy (3 to 4 minutes). Gradually whisk hot cream into beaten egg yolks. Return mixture to saucepan; stir in vanilla. Cook over medium heat, stirring constantly, until custard reaches 160°F and is thick enough to coat back of metal spoon (4 to 5 minutes). (Do not boil because egg yolks will curdle.) Refrigerate 8 hours or overnight. Remove truffle dessert from pan by lifting the aluminum foil. Remove aluminum foil. Slice truffle dessert with hot knife into 16 slices. Spoon about 1 tablespoon custard onto individual dessert plates; place slice of truffle dessert over custard. Garnish with finely chopped hazelnuts. **YIELD:** 16 servings.

Nutrition Information (1 serving): Calories 380; Protein 4g; Carbohydrate 26g; Fat 31g; Cholesterol 145mg; Sodium 45mg.

Simple Mini Cocoa Cheesecakes

These chocolate cheesecakes make a lovely addition to any holiday dessert tray and can easily be made ahead.

Preparation time: 30 minutes • Baking time: 38 minutes • Chilling time: 2 hours

Crust
12 (2-inch) foil backing cups
12 vanilla wafer cookies

Cheesecake
1/2 cup sugar
1/4 cup unsweetened cocoa
2 (8 ounce) packages cream
   cheese, softened
2 eggs
1 teaspoon vanilla

Topping
1 cup LAND O LAKES®
   Sour Cream
2 tablespoons sugar
1 teaspoon vanilla

Garnish
Chocolate curls, if desired
Cut-up fruit, if desired
Powdered sugar, if desired

Heat oven to 325°. Line 12-cup muffin pan with foil baking cups; place 1 cookie in each foil cup.

In large mixer bowl combine 1/2 cup sugar, cocoa, cream cheese, eggs and 1 teaspoon vanilla. Beat at medium speed, scraping bowl often, until smooth (2 to 3 minutes). Pour over each cookie, filling cups 3/4 full. Bake for 30 minutes.

Meanwhile, in small bowl stir together all topping ingredients. Spoon about 1 tablespoon topping onto each hot cheesecake. Continue baking for 8 to 10 minutes or until set. Cool; remove from pan. Cover; refrigerate until firm (1 to 2 hours).

To serve, garnish with chocolate curls, fruit and powdered sugar. Store refrigerated. **YIELD:** 12 servings.

Nutrition Facts (1 serving): Calories 200; Protein 6g; Carbohydrate 18g; Fat 12g; Cholesterol 70mg; Sodium 200mg

Chocolate Raspberry Mousse

Serve this delicious chocolate raspberry mousse
in pretty parfait glasses.

Preparation time: 20 minutes

1/2 cup
   LAND O LAKES® Butter,
   softened
1/3 cup sugar
2 (1 ounce) squares semi-sweet
   baking chocolate, melted,
   cooled
1/2 cup refrigerated
   pasteurized liquid egg
2 teaspoons raspberry
   liqueur, if desired
1 cup fresh raspberries

In small mixer bowl combine butter and sugar. Beat at medium speed, scraping bowl often, until very light and fluffy (2 to 3 minutes). Add chocolate; continue beating, scraping bowl often, until well mixed (1 to 2 minutes). Add egg; continue beating, scraping bowl often, until very light and fluffy (4 to 5 minutes). By hand, stir in raspberry liqueur. To serve, place several raspberries in bottom of each of 4 parfait glasses. Top with 1/4 cup chocolate mousse. Add several more raspberries. Top with 1/4 cup chocolate mousse. Garnish with raspberries. Store refrigerated. **YIELD:** 4 servings.

Nutrition Information (1 serving): Calories 400; Protein 4g; Carbohydrate 30g; Fat 31g; Cholesterol 85mg; Sodium 295mg.

Layered Pralines & Cream

*A crunchy praline mixture complements this
creamy custard.*

*Preparation time: 30 minutes • Baking time: 14 minutes • Cooling time: 30 minutes • Cooking time: 10 minutes
Chilling time: 2 hours*

Crunch Mixture

1/4 cup
  LAND O LAKES® Butter

1/2 cup bite-size crispy rice
  cereal squares

1/2 cup flaked coconut

1/2 cup slivered almonds

1/2 cup firmly packed
  brown sugar

1/2 cup chopped pecans

Custard

1/2 cup sugar

1 cup milk

1 egg, slightly beaten

1 tablespoon cornstarch

1 teaspoon vanilla

1 cup whipping cream,
  whipped

Heat oven to 325°. In 15x10x1-inch jelly roll pan melt butter in oven (4 to 5 minutes). Add remaining crunch mixture ingredients; stir well to coat. Bake for 12 to 14 minutes, stirring occasionally, until golden brown. Cool completely; crumble cereal with fingers. In 2-quart saucepan combine all custard ingredients <u>except</u> vanilla and whipped cream. Cook over medium heat, stirring often, until mixture comes to a full boil (7 to 9 minutes). Boil 1 minute. Remove from heat; stir in vanilla. Cover surface with plastic food wrap; refrigerate until cooled completely (1 to 2 hours). Fold whipped cream into custard mixture. Just before serving, alternate layers of custard and crunch mixture into dessert glasses. **YIELD:** 6 servings.

*Nutrition Information (1 serving): Calories 540; Protein 6g; Carbohydrate 48g; Fat 38g;
Cholesterol 114mg; Sodium 150mg.*

Chocolate Truffle Pudding

Indulge in this truffle-like pudding to satisfy
chocolate cravings.

Preparation time: 15 minutes • Cooking time: 15 minutes • Cooling time: 30 minutes • Chilling time: 2 hours

1 cup milk

1 cup whipping cream

1/2 cup sugar

3 tablespoons unsweetened
   cocoa

2 tablespoons cornstarch

3/4 cup semi-sweet real
   chocolate chips

1 egg, slightly beaten

2 egg yolks, slightly beaten

2 tablespoons
   LAND O LAKES® Butter

1 teaspoon vanilla

Sweetened whipped cream

Zest of orange peel

Unsweetened cocoa

In 2-quart saucepan stir together milk and whipping cream. Cook over medium heat until warm (3 to 5 minutes). In small bowl stir together sugar, 3 tablespoons cocoa and cornstarch. Gradually add to milk mixture. Add all remaining ingredients <u>except</u> whipped cream, zest of orange peel and cocoa. Continue cooking, stirring constantly, until pudding just begins to thicken (5 to 10 minutes). Pour pudding into 6 or 8 (1/2 cup) individual dessert dishes. Cool 30 minutes. Cover; refrigerate at least 2 hours. Pipe with sweetened whipped cream; top with zest of orange peel and sprinkle with cocoa. **YIELD:** 8 servings.

Nutrition Information (1 serving): Calories 310; Protein 4g; Carbohydrate 27g; Fat 23g;
Cholesterol 130mg; Sodium 80mg.

Orange Creme Caramel

*Rich, velvety custard forms its own caramel
sauce as it bakes.*

Preparation time: 45 minutes • Baking time: 45 minutes • Standing time: 30 minutes

1/2 cup sugar

2 1/2 cups milk

1/3 cup sugar

3 eggs

1 tablespoon orange flavored
   liqueur <u>or</u> orange juice

Nutmeg

Pear, red apple,
   nectarine <u>or</u> berries

Orange flavored liqueur
   <u>or</u> orange juice

Heat oven to 350°. In 1-quart saucepan cook 1/2 cup sugar over medium heat, stirring constantly, until golden brown and forms a caramel syrup (6 to 8 minutes). Divide caramel syrup between 6 (6 ounce) custard cups or fluted ramekins. Let stand 10 minutes. Meanwhile, in 2-quart saucepan heat milk over medium heat, stirring occasionally, until hot (4 to 5 minutes). (Do not boil.) In medium bowl, with wire whisk, gradually stir sugar into eggs; gradually whisk hot milk into egg mixture. Stir in 1 tablespoon orange flavored liqueur. Pour about <u>1/2 cup</u> milk mixture into each custard cup; sprinkle with nutmeg. Place custard cups in 13x9-inch baking pan; pour 2 inches hot water into pan. Bake for 40 to 45 minutes or until knife inserted in center of custards comes out clean. Let stand 30 minutes. Serve warm or cover; refrigerate. Just before serving, cut choice of fruit into very thin slices; sprinkle with orange flavored liqueur. On individual dessert plates unmold creme caramel; garnish with sliced fruit or berries. **YIELD:** 6 servings.

Nutrition Information (1 serving): Calories 200; Protein 7g; Carbohydrate 35g; Fat 5g; Cholesterol 115mg; Sodium 83mg.

216

Chocolate Caramel Fudge Sauce

A rich and creamy fudge sauce featuring milk chocolate chips, caramels and half-and-half.

Preparation time: 30 minutes

20 caramels, unwrapped
1 1/2 cups real milk
   chocolate chips
1/2 cup half-and-half
2 tablespoons
   LAND O LAKES® Butter

In 2-quart saucepan combine all ingredients. Cook over medium low heat, stirring often, until caramels and chocolate are melted and mixture is smooth (10 to 20 minutes). Serve warm over ice cream or cake. **YIELD:** 1 1/2 cups.

Nutrition Information (1 tablespoon): Calories 100; Protein 1g; Carbohydrate 12g; Fat 6g; Cholesterol 5mg; Sodium 40mg.

Flavored Coffees

The perfect way to end a delightful meal
— a cup of flavored coffee.

(pictured)

Weak Coffee
1 tablespoon coffee
3/4 cup (6 ounces) water*

Medium Coffee
2 tablespoons coffee
3/4 cup (6 ounces) water*

Strong Coffee
3 tablespoons coffee
3/4 cup (6 ounces) water*

For flavored coffees, start with strong brewed coffee.

* Use freshly drawn cold water; do not use softened water.

Irish Coffee: Stir in Irish whiskey and sugar to taste.
Top with sweetened whipped cream.

Almond Coffee: Stir in almond flavored liqueur to taste.
Top with sweetened whipped cream and toasted sliced almonds.
For non-alcoholic Almond Coffee use medium brewed coffee.
Stir in almond extract and sugar to taste. Top with sweetened
whipped cream and toasted sliced almonds.

Mexican Coffee: Stir in coffee flavored liqueur to taste. Top with
sweetened whipped cream; sprinkle with brown sugar and cinnamon.

Chocolate Coffee: Stir in chocolate flavored syrup and cream
to taste.

Iced Coffee: Cool coffee; serve over ice. Stir in sugar, cream and/or
milk to taste, if desired.

Coffee 'N Cream: Stir in your favorite flavor ice cream to taste.

Coffee Condiments
To be used as condiments with hot brewed coffee: Chocolate curls,
grated orange peel, orange slices, cinnamon sticks, sweetened
whipped cream, brown sugar and your favorite liqueurs.

Spicy Whipped Cream
Serve dolloped on hot brewed coffee.

> **1 cup whipping cream**
> **2 tablespoons powdered sugar**
> **1/4 teaspoon cinnamon**
> **Dash nutmeg**

In chilled small mixer bowl beat chilled whipping cream at high
speed, scraping bowl often, until soft peaks form. Continue beating,
gradually adding powdered sugar, cinnamon and nutmeg, until stiff
peaks form. **YIELD:** 1 1/2 cups.

Index